THE LIFE OF
Mr Silas Told

Engraved after the original picture in the sequence 'Industry and Idleness' by William Hogarth

'WHEN WE WERE IN THE CART . . . I SAID TO HIM, "ARE YOU AFRAID TO DIE?"'

THE LIFE OF

Mr Silas Told

WRITTEN BY HIMSELF

WITH A NOTE TO
The Serious & Candid Reader
BY JOHN WESLEY, A.M.

London
THE EPWORTH PRESS

THE EPWORTH PRESS
(FRANK H. CUMBERS)
25-35 City Road, London, E.C.1

MELBOURNE   CAPE TOWN
NEW YORK   TORONTO

First published 1786
This edition 1954

SET IN MONOTYPE CASLON AND PRINTED IN
GREAT BRITAIN BY THE CAMELOT PRESS LTD.
LONDON AND SOUTHAMPTON

Contents

—Repentance and Conversion—In the Cart with Condemned Men on the Way to Execution—Testimonies to the power of Divine Grace—Visits Prisons and Workhouses in and about London—Unbelief—"Lord, it is enough."

To the Reader

MR. SILAS TOLD was a man of good understanding, although not much indebted to education. In his life are many remarkable instances of divine Providence, some of which are of an extraordinary kind; yet we may easily credit them, if we consider, on the one hand, that he was a person of eminent veracity, and on the other, that he relates what he saw with his own eyes, and heard with his own ears. I believe those very passages will be of use to serious and candid readers.

JOHN WESLEY

City-road, Nov. 8, 1789

Chapter One

I WAS born at the Lime-Kilns, near the Hotwells, in the city of Bristol, on the 3d day of April, 1711. My parents were very creditable people. My grandfather Told, who was an eminent Physician at London, was possessed of a very plentiful estate in houses: my grandmother also enjoyed a very considerable fortune, at Torrington, in the west of England, worth about £600 per annum; but, having a great dislike to London, and her husband's business fixing him there, caused so far a separation between them, that their posterity experienced very fatal consequences therefrom, as he took to him a housekeeper, who as I was informed by my mother, when she found a fair opportunity, gave him what proved his end, and secured all his writings, and the title-deeds of the estate, together with all the ready money, plate, jewels, &c.; the family being absent from London. And although she could not hold the estate, yet, for a great number of years, and even to this day, several people have lived rent-free, for want of proper title-deeds to empower the heir to receive the same.

When I first came to London, after faithfully serving my time to Captain Moses Lilly, of Bristol, on the seas, I was advised to make claim to the estate; but for want of money to go to law, together with the loss of the writings, I declined it; and gave up all hopes of being profited thereby: and as to my grandmother Told's estate in the west, this never came within my knowledge.

My father was a Physician at Bristol, and in great esteem throughout the city; but being a great schemer, it proved his ruin, and the impoverishing of his family. One instance, was, the building a wet dock at the Lime-Kilns, where I was born; where he laid out thirty-three hundred pounds, and lost every penny, by one Evans, for whom my father undertook the business, who failed, and went off: this laid my father under the necessity of going out doctor of a Guineaman, in the course of which voyage he died, leaving only six hundred pounds for the maintenance and education of five children.

My mother was born at Topsham, near Exeter, and was daughter to Captain Thomas Suckabitch, otherwise Sucksbury, who commanded a ship upwards for forty years. Something remarkable is related of my mother's pedigree; in tracing which up to the farthest knowledge, it has been represented, that one of the Kings of the West Angles, being out on a certain day hunting with his nobles, discovered a male child in the wood, with no one near it but a large bitch; the maid having left the child with the bitch, whilst she went a nutting in the woods. The King, who found the child sucking the bitch, carried it home, named it Suckabitch, and brought him up, giving him a large estate round the spot where he was found, which the succeeding generations have severally enjoyed to this day, but altered to that of Sucksbury.

My brother Joseph and sister Dulcy, with myself, were sent to nurse at Kingswood, near Bristol, where we were taken care of by the most tender-hearted woman I ever met with. At this place we all continued till I arrived at the age of eight years; my friends at Bristol then made interest for me to be admitted into the hospital of Edward Colson, Esq., on St. Augustine's Back, near the quay of Bristol: a school, I dare venture to say, that cannot be surpassed by any throughout Great Britain for piety and Christian discipline, having a Minister to attend twice a week regularly, for the instruction of one hundred boys in their duty towards God and man.

Here it may not be improper to give an impartial account of the character and piety of this worthy benefactor; and also of the wisdom and goodness of Almighty God in raising up so useful a man to posterity. He was the son of Edward Colson, a journeyman soap-boiler, whose wages did not exceed ten shillings per week. He had ten children then living, of whom Edward was the eldest, who, when he had arrived at an age fit to be put an apprentice, was bound to a Virginia Captain, about the time that the colonists were transported to North America. This proved his first rise, as his behaviour and humble readiness to obey his superiors moved many of the merchants, who first settled there, to make Edward, the cabin-boy, many presents; insomuch, that before his ship departed from America for England he had acquired the sum of fifty pounds; and being of an exceeding liberal disposition, on his arrival at Bristol, he hastened with the fifty pounds, and dispersed every farthing thereof to the prisoners in Newgate. Shortly after, he sailed again to Virginia, where, through the kind providence of God, he gathered among his former friends twice the money of the preceding voyage, and disposed of the whole after the same manner.

At the age of forty years he became a very eminent East-India merchant, prior to the incorporation of the East-India Company, and had forty sail of ships of his own, with immense riches flowing in upon him. He still remained uniform in his charitable disposition, distributing many thousand pounds to various charities in and about London, besides private gifts in many parts of the kingdom. In the year 1708 he instituted a very magnificent school on St.

Augustine's Back, in Bristol which cost him eleven thousand pounds in the building; and endowed the same with between seventeen and eighteen hundred pounds per annum, for ever. He likewise gave ten pounds for apprenticing every boy; and for twelve years after his death, ten pounds to put them into business. He maintained religious economy in the school, such as prayers three times a day, performed by one of the senior boys. He also caused to be erected a very grand almshouse, with an elegant chapel situated in the front thereof, at St. Michael's-Hill, Bristol, for twenty-four old men, with a handsome allowance for every individual, and a Clergyman to attend them weekly.

He founded a large free-school in Temple-street, Bristol, which was set apart for the education and clothing of forty boys; and likewise provided for ten old men in the city almshouse. I do not recollect any church throughout that city, where a memorandum of his donations to several useful charities is not recorded. I have been likewise informed that he built, at his own expense, the whole church and town of All-Saints, near the Tolsey, Bristol; together with many other public charities now extant in that city.

It has been frequently reported that his private charities far exceeded those in public. I have heard that one of his ships, trading to the East Indies, had been missing upwards of three years, and was supposed to be destroyed at sea; but at length she arrived, richly laden. When his principal clerk brought him the report of her arrival, and of the riches on board, he said, as she was totally given up for lost, he would by no means claim any right to her: therefore he ordered the ship and merchandises to be sold, and the produce thereof to be applied towards the relief of the needy; which directions were immediately carried into execution.

Another singular instance of his tender consciousness for charity was at the age of forty, when he entertained some thoughts of changing his condition. He paid his addresses to a lady; but being very timorous lest he should be hindered in his pious and charitable designs, he was determined to make a Christian trial of her temper and disposition, and, therefore, one morning filled his pockets full of gold and silver, in order that if any object presented itself in the course of their tour over London-bridge, he might satisfy his intentions. While they were walking near St. Agnes' church, a woman in extreme misery, with twins in her lap, sat begging; and as he and his intended lady were arm in arm, he beheld the wretched object, put his hand in his pocket, and took out a handful of gold and silver, casting it into the poor woman's lap. The lady being greatly alarmed at such a profuse generosity, coloured prodigiously; so that when they were gone a little farther towards the bridge foot, she turned to him, and said, "Sir, do you know what you did a few minutes ago?" "Madam," replied Mr. Colson, "I never let my right hand know what my left hand doeth." He then took his leave of her, and for this reason never married to the day of his death, although he lived to the age of 83.

In the year 1721 he died at Mortlake, up the river Thames, having left many considerable legacies to charitable uses. Providentially I was in the school at the time of his death, when orders were given for all the children to be learned by heart the 90th Psalm, to sing before the corpse as it entered the city, which was at Lawford's-Gate, where we joined the hearse, and sung before it the space of five hours, amidst a most numerous and crowded audience. It is impossible to describe in what manner the houses and streets were lined with all ranks of people; and although the rain descended in torrents, none paid any regard thereto; but the whole multitude seemed determined to see the last of so eminent a man. We came at last to All-Saints' church, where he was interred under the communion-table. The day of his birth, and also of his death, are commemorated to this day throughout the city of Bristol. His many donations to the poor are, by his executors, faithfully upheld still.

I now proceed to give an account of my life from my

infancy, as far as it may be brought to my remembrance, which is from three years of age. When I was in petticoats, my sister Dulcybella and I wandered often into the woods and fields, fixing ourselves under the hedges, conversing about God and happiness; so that at times I have been transported in such a measure with heavenly bliss, that whether in the body or out of the body, I could not tell: this happiness attended me for a few years.

Once, when we were very young, we wandered into Kingswood, and lost ourselves in the woods, and were in the utmost consternation, lest we should be devoured by the wild beasts; but quickly the kind providence of God permitted a large dog to come behind us; although no house was within a mile, yet the dog drove us clear out of the wood to a place we knew, and never barked at us! And when we now looked around to behold the dog, he was not to be seen. Being heedless, we wandered again into the woods, and were a second time bewildered, and in greater perplexity than before; when on a sudden, looking around, we beheld the same dog making towards us, and he came directly upon us; and we, being much terrified, ran from him, until we got a second time into our knowledge; nor did he leave us till we were driven by him where we could not run into any more labyrinths. I then turned about to look for the dog, but saw no more of him, although we were upon an open common. Surely this was the Lord's doing, and it is marvellous in our eyes.

Chapter Two

IN the year 1725 I was bound an apprentice to Captain Moses Lilly, in the ship Prince of Wales, and sailed from Bristol, for Cork and Jamaica, in the month of July.

Here my sufferings began: being wrought on by the Spirit of God, and totally ignorant of the maxims of the world, and having been six years in the hospital, free from all intercourse with mankind, a sea life was very disagreeable to me. The first reception I met with on board, when the ship lay in King-road, was this: the chief Mate called the cabin-boy; but he not being on board, he sent me to the cook to get him a plate of victuals, which I really imagined was meant for myself; and accordingly got a plate full, carried it down into the cabin, and having a keen appetite, made a very comfortable dinner. When the chief Mate had done his business, he sent for me in order to bring his victuals. I told him I understood it was for myself, and that I had eat it up; upon which he knocked me down, and began cursing and d——ning me at a horrible rate. This language I was never acquainted with, therefore I thought I should have broken my heart with grief; and having no friend to whom I could apply for redress, I was forced to suffer repeated acts of barbarity, which continued for eleven years.

The first of my sufferings was seasickness, which held me till our arrival at Jamaica. After lying at Kingston many months, (not having any freight for England,) the ship made a voyage down to the Bay of Campeachy, in the Spanish West Indies; at which place she lay at anchor about twelve miles from the land, where, with her bottom beating the ground every swell of the sea, she was exceedingly damaged. When we had completed her cargo, we sailed back for Jamaica, very short of all sorts of provision, expecting to have a short passage; but, to our mortification, it was a passage of fourteen weeks. After being out three weeks, we were put to short allowance, both of bread and water; one biscuit and two-thirds of a pint of water per day. This was what I never before experienced, and therefore it was the more grievous to be sustained; and had it not been for a heavy shower of rain, off the island of Cuba, we must have perished for want. Here we stopped up all the scuppers, and saved about six casks of water, by the use of the swabs, which we dried the decks with, and which we wrung into the casks; and although the water was very bitter, yet, providentially, our lives were preserved thereby; for we were reduced to half a pint of water a day, and that full of mud and maggots; yet were we three days before we arrived at Blue-Fields, the west end of Jamaica, without a single pint of water on board, having been eleven weeks destitute of biscuit, peas, or flour; so that we had neither food to eat, nor water to drink.

When we came to an anchor in Blue-Fields Bay, we hoisted out the long boat, stowed her full of casks, and despatched her for fresh water, when one of our men fell flat upon his belly, and drank so immoderately, that a few hours after he came on board he expired; and the next morning we sewed him up in a hammock, and threw him overboard, when a large shark descended after him, and, we supposed, swallowed the whole body.

As we were riding at anchor in Kingston harbour, the capital of Jamaica, waiting for a freight for England, a very great noise was heard in the atmosphere, similar to that of splitting wood, and the elements were much disturbed. Our chief Mate was of an opinion, that we should be visited by a hurricane that evening; which began about eight o'clock the same night, and held, without intermission, till six o'clock the following evening. All language fails me to set forth the violence of this tempest, as nothing could stand before it. There were in the harbour of Kingston seventy-six sail of ships, many of which were very large; but all riding with three anchors a-head; and notwithstanding ours was a new ship, with three new cables and anchors, yet, about four o'clock in the morning, we parted all three cables at once, and turning broadside to the wind, over-set and sunk to the ground. In that condition we were driven, with our gunnel to the bottom, down to the extremity of the harbour, which is about twelve miles. Though we were the first ship that drove from her anchors, yet all our masts stood; but this was not the situation of any vessel beside, for the whole fleet lost all their masts, yards, and bowsprits, and every vessel, large or small, was driven, with astonishing rapidity, high on the land.

The same hurricane drove a large snow, of two hundred and twenty tons, above half a mile into the country, which broke and tore the cocoa-nut trees up by the roots; likewise a very heavy brigantine was cast upon the wharfs in the town, and a large sloop, of about one hundred tons, lay with her keep across the brig's deck. In short, that part of the town nearest the water side was barricaded with the wrecks of ships and vessels; and as there were no tides to ebb and flood, consequently there was no possibility of getting them off; nor were there any, save one fine stately ship, which rode out that tempest: so that seventy-five sail of ships of war and merchantmen were inevitably destroyed in the tremendous overthrow.

One remarkable instance I would take notice of; viz., the ship Nicholson, Captain Smiler, of London, quite a new and beautiful vessel, sunk at her anchors, and all on board perished, except the Captain's son and four more, who were saved by getting into a small boat, called the Moses, that carried no more than one hogshead of sugar at a time.

All the ships at Port-Royal shared the same fate with those at Kingston, except the Winchelsea man-of-war, and Kirkington, of Bristol, Captain Pills, both of which cut away their masts, and were upon the brink of foundering even at the close of the hurricane, which was on Saturday evening, about six o'clock. Here I would briefly observe how suddenly the storm ceased; it varied from east to west, and was for a few hours calm; after which it chopped round to its former point, and blowing with a vehemence impossible to be expressed, lasted near an hour, and was succeeded by a second calm. Two or three days after the destruction of these parts of the island, viz., Kingston and Port-Royal, and likewise of the dreadful consequences of the storm upon the fleet of ships, the drowned seamen were driven upon the shores for miles down the harbour, and were left to be devoured by the crows and other wild fowl.

Immediately after the hurricane, followed a pestilential sickness, which swept away thousands of the natives: every morning I observed between thirty and forty corpses carried past my window; and being very near death myself, I expected every day the messenger of my dissolution. From this illness, I contracted an habitual fever and ague, which continued eleven months, so that I was wasted to a mere shadow; nor had I one person under heaven to take care of me, except a negro, who brought me every day a dose of Jesuit's bark to the warehouse, where I was laid in a hammock.

A length my master gave me up, and I wandered up and down the town, almost parched with the insufferable blaze of the sun, till I was resolved to lay me down and die, as I had neither money nor friend. Accordingly, I fixed upon a dunghill on the east end of the town of Kingston; and being in so weak a condition, I pondered much upon Job's case, and considered mine similar to that of his. However, I was fully resigned to death, nor had I the slightest expectations of relief from any quarter; yet the kind providence of God was over me, and raised up a friend in an entire stranger. A London Captain coming by, was struck with the shocking object, came up to me, and, in a very compassionate manner, asked me if I had any friend upon the island of whom I could obtain relief. He likewise asked me to whom I belonged. I answered, to Captain Moses Lilly, and had been cast away in the late hurricane.

This Captain having some knowledge of my master, and cursing him for a barbarous villain, told me, he would compel him to take proper care of me. In about a quarter of an hour my master arrived, (whom I had not seen before for six weeks,) and took me to a public house kept by a Mrs. Hutchinson, and there ordered me to be taken proper care of. However, he soon quitted the island, and directed his course for England, leaving me behind; and ordered me, if I recovered, to take my passage for England in the Mont-serrat, Captain David Jones, a very tenderhearted man: this was the first alleviation of my misery. The Captain sent his son on shore, in order to receive me on board; and when I came along-side, standing on the ship's gunnel, he addressed me in a very humane and compassionate manner, to the following effect: "Come, poor child, into the cabin, and you shall want nothing the ship affords; go, and my son shall pre-pare for you, in the first place, a basin of good egg-flip and any thing else that may be conducive to your relief." But being still very ill with my fever and ague, I could neither eat nor drink.

Captain Jones sent for the boatswain, and asked him if he knew any remedy for an intermitting fever. He told the Captain, that he could procure a remedy, that if I lived fifty years longer, I should not be subject to it any more. This was in the year 1727, which is now forty-eight years ago, and I do not remember to have experienced one fit of it since; and, although I had been afflicted with the ague eleven months, the boatswain cured me in less than five hours. Here I began immediately to recover my strength, and become more lively and active than ever I had been.

Upon our sailing for Bristol, Captain Jones, being of a free, affable temper, in order to please the ship's company, steered his course to make the island of Bermudas. Upon our arrival there, we scudded along shore from one end of the island to the other; nor did I perceive either hill or mountain upon the whole island, it being fine, level, grassy land. After we lost sight of this island, we made the best of our passage for England; but in the prosecution thereof, something rather supernatural happened, and, I suppose, will not be easily credited by my readers. Be that as it may, my intentions are not to advance beyond the bounds of truth, in relating the following circumstance, or in any other throughout this tract.

In the space of five weeks after our departure from Bermudas, the Captain ordered the man to keep a sharp lookout at the fore-top-mast-head, as by our journal and calculation of the log-book, we expected to be no great distance from Cape Clear, the west end of Ireland. Accordingly, one morning, about seven o'clock, the sentinel at the mast-head threw out the signal for land, about two points on the weather-bow; but as, at that time, the ship was running with the wind on the star-board-beam, the Captain deemed it most advisable to brace all sharp up, and lie as near the wind as we possibly could. The land soon became conspicuous to the naked eye from the deck, and we altered our course as the land edged round, but would not attempt to make any nearer approach towards it than a full league. I frequently had my eye fixed upon the land, as had also the Captain and all the ship's company, while we were at work clearing the decks, bending the cables, and making ourselves ready, in all respects, to adapt the ship for anchorages, or to be prepared for running into a harbour, in case of emergency. I do not remember ever to have seen any place apparently more fertile, or better cultivated; the fields seeming to be covered with verdure, and very beautiful; and as the surf of the sea almost convinced us that it was playing on the shore, we were beyond all doubt for the space of ten hours. Our Captain, therefore, gave the man who first discovered it, ten gallons of rum and twenty pounds of sugar; but about six o'clock in the evening, as we were washing the decks, and the sun was shining clear from the westward, in less than a minute, we lost all sight of the land; nothing but the horizon, interspersed with a few pale clouds, was perceptible from the deck. This filled the ship's company with the utmost astonishment; nor did we make the coast of Ireland for several days after. Our Captain and ship's company concluded that it was Old Brazille, which navigators affirm to have been destroyed by an earthquake between five and six hundred years ago.

Chapter Three

AT length we arrived at Bristol, and I was with my master, Captain Moses Lilly, a few weeks, when he consigned me over to Timothy Tucker, Commander of the Royal George, bound for Guinea and the West Indies. A greater villain, I firmly believe, never existed.

The first demonstration of his notorious conduct was the enforcement of a white woman out of her native country, and selling her to the black Prince of Bonny, on the African coast. The next proof of his villany was the vile and blasphemous language wherewith he perpetually governed the seamen. A third instance of his horrid conduct was particularly noticed one Sunday morning. As I went down to the gun-room, in order to procure necessary provisions for the ship's company, the Captain happened to find me at the bread cask, and declared that I was taking from thence considerably more than would be used; therefore he went immediately to the cabin, and brought out with him his large horse-whip, and exercised it about my body in so unmerciful a manner, that not only the clothes on my back were cut to pieces, but every sailor on board declared they could see my bones. Yet this act of barbarity did not give him sufficient satisfaction; for he threw me all along the deck, and jumped many times upon the pit of my stomach; and had not the people laid hold of my two legs, and thrown me under the windlass, (after the manner they threw dead cats or dogs,) he would have ended his despotic cruelty in murder. Repeated instances of this behaviour were committed by him on the principal part of his seamen in the course of his voyage.

One day I accompanied the King Arigo on shore for the benefit of my health, (as the savage Captain had almost put an end to my life,) and continued there for the space of six weeks, and slept with the King's son, Prince Arigo, during the same. At this place, the black King had six hundred concubines, thirty of whom dwelt in his house, and an elderly woman presided over the rest. One morning in particular, I was suddenly seized with a racking pain in my head; I acquainted the Queen in Moorish, with the cause of my indisposition; she informed his black Majesty therewith, who ordered me some "doctor," as they term it; and about half-a-dozen of his ladies took me into a back yard, and stripped me quite naked, even to my skin, set me on a joint-stool, and gave me some yabba, (or water,) with a cloth to dry myself. I could not conceive what they purposed doing with me, as the elder lady invented divers stratagems to get me into a studious frame of mind. When they perceived me quite fixed, looking at my feet, and apprehensive they were about to wash them with the hot water, suddenly the female monitor, or president, snatched the cloth out of the water, and threw it directly in my face, which startled me to such a degree that it effectually removed the pain in an instant. Here I penetrated their maxims in performing the cure.

However, in about half an hour's time my pain revisited my head with greater violence than before; and I informed the Queen that *ishe* was *obagona*, or my head was very bad: she then told his Majesty that my disorder was returned, who immediately collected his grandy-men together, and they carried me to the top of a very high hill, on the right hand side of which was situated the King's palaver-house, or place erected for their heathenish worship. They took with them a dog, and about a hundred roots called yams. When I entered the house, I was struck with uncommon amazement at the sight of forty or fifty black men's heads hanged around this palaver-house. Here I was inexpressibly terrified, as I had received a very pious and Christian education; so that their diabolical and gross proceedings created great horror upon my soul. At length, they commenced the usual sacrifices to their gods; during which, one of the senior characters, who signalised himself by a scimitar at his side, drew it, took the dog before mentioned, laid it on the floor, and, at one blow, cut off his head. He then pulled the tongue out of its mouth, fastened it beneath his teeth, and instantly came and touched my forehead, cheeks, chin, and every joint with the dog's tongue.

The King, finding these means to be ineffectual, proceeded further, and directed some of his people to sprinkle the dust with a quantity of palm-wine, and to lead me through a trackless desert down to the ship, conceiving the wine (as there was no water to be had) might create a path to the sea-shore. This answered, and Prince Arigo, the King's son, hailed the ship, which lay at a small distance from land, and desired them to send the boat on shore, as *piccaninni baccaneau* was *yarre, yarre*, that is, "was very sick." Accordingly it was done; and when I came on board, Tucker, with a grim countenance, and horrid expressions, asked me what ailed me. I replied that I had a strong fever on me. "Then," said he, "I will soon cure you;" so he went and brought his horse-whip, and although I was extremely sick he whipped me unmercifully: however, his medicine did not perform the cure, but heightened my fever, so that I was nearly brought to the gates of death; yet God raised me up again. Upon our arrival at St. Thomas's the European woman, whom Tucker brought out from England, died in a shocking manner, was sewed up in a hammock, and thrown overboard, with a bag of ballast at her feet, in order to sink her; but in the course of a week, the corpse of the woman was observed to float upon the water. I believe God had suffered this uncommon circumstance to happen, in order to open the eyes of our wicked Captain; but he had no remorse.

I cannot but give one instance more of the barbarity of this Captain during the voyage, and his gross manner of executing it, as a more bloody and inhuman action surely never was perpetrated by an Englishman. This was upon one of our black slaves, who through a violent sickness, was worn to a mere skeleton; and as he could not eat his allowance, the savage (Tucker) invented a scheme to compel him to eat, and laid to his charge that he was sulky: however, the poor creature could not. Upon this, the Captain called for his black cabin-boy, Robin, to bring him his horsewhip; he did so, and Tucker began lashing the poor sick man, till, I firmly believe, from his neck to his ankles, there was nothing to be seen but blood and wounds. The poor creature made no kind of resistance, nor spoke one word: this provoked our blood-thirsty wretch, so that he went still farther, and told him in Negroish, he would *tickeravoo* him. The poor slave answered, "*Adomma*," which signified, "So be it."

By this time, the Captain's dinner was ready under the awning of the quarter-deck; he left the man in shocking agonies, bleeding and groaning on the fore-castle, came to his dinner like a hog, and eat without fear or shame. After he had dined, he called John Lad, and ordered him to get two ammunition pistols well loaded with ball; then called for Robin the cabin-boy, to bring them forward, which when done, he left his table, and ordered John Lad to follow him, which he accordingly did, with one pistol in each hand. They both went forward on the main-deck; the poor object sat with his back against the larboard gunnel of the ship. Then Tucker, with a virulent grin, pointing one of the pistols to him, told him it would kill him. The man replied, as before "*Adomma*." Upon this the Captain applied the mouth of the pistol to the middle of his forehead, and fired. The man instantly clapped his hands to his head, one behind, and the other before, and stared the Captain in the face, the blood gushing from his forehead, but he did not fall. Tucker then turning to John Lad, with a blasphemous oath, said, "This will not kill him;" and immediately clapped another to his ear, and fired that also; nor did he drop even then. At last the Captain ordered John Lad to fire another through his heart, which when done, he dropped down dead.

All the men slaves, in consequence of this uncommon murder, rose upon the ship's company, with full purpose to slay us all; but we nimbly betaking ourselves to the cannon, pointed them through a bulk-head, that parted the main and quarter deck; which when they perceived, the greater part of them ran down between decks, and the remainder jumped overboard, and were all drowned save one or two, which, with the assistance of the boat, we rescued from the violence of the sea. At length we arrived at Barbadoes, when Captain Tucker's notorious conduct was repressed in some measure, which was visibly perceived by the sending the slaves large quantities of rum and sugar. Yet, on his leaving that island, he renewed his former cruelties; but did not exercise them on me with that degree of severity which he had used in the passage to Kingston.

In the course of eight weeks, we arrived at Bristol. My original master (Moses Lilly) received all my wages, but allowed me no pocket money; and fitted me out very scantily for the next voyage. Having no friend or relation in London, I was drawn in to perform another voyage with Tucker; (the bare idea of which almost broke my heart;) yet he treated me with less rigour than in the voyage before.

I have two circumstances to remark in this voyage: the first was, when slaved and ready to sail for Bonny, we dropped down, and came to anchor a little without the bar. About twelve o'clock at night, an universal shriek was heard among the slaves between decks; and being asked what ailed them, they with wild confusion, said, that *egbo*, or the devil, was among them. The next morning, when we came to open the hatches, to admit the air into their loathsome dens, and for the purpose of discharging their tubs, to our great surprise, we found a number of them lying dead. Upon hoisting about eighty of them, we saved thirty-nine, and the rest, having irrecoverably lost their breath in the suffocation, the Captain directed us to cast them overboard, which was instantly done.

A second circumstance which happened on board our ship, was the Captain's inhuman cruelty to the ship's cook. The poor man had nothing but green wood to make his furnace boil with, on which account it was impossible for him to get the food ready in time. For this the Captain horse-whipped him, and stabbed him in the face, so that the poor man's life was grievously burdensome to him. Indeed he oftentimes hinted that he would throw himself overboard; but we endeavoured to dissuade him from it. At last, one morning, about eight o'clock, he plunged into the sea without our knowledge. When we informed the captain of it, he answered, with some degree of pleasure, that he saw a hat swimming astern, which he supposed was the b———d of a b———'s.

After this I was shipped on board the Scipio, Captain Roach, who was a well-tempered gentleman, and very free with all his ship's company; but having purchased a black girl for his own use, she in the end proved the cause of his death. One evening as we lay at anchor in New Calabar, one Tom Ancora came on board who talked very good English. Captain Roach, having made a tub of punch on the quarter-deck, had the fiddler and the ship's company dancing with him, but left me with Tom Ancora to purchase the slaves. When this was done, Tom desired me to give him a dram, which I did; he then desired me to let the bottle stand; I told him I must first obtain the Captain's leave. I then went to Captain Roach, who gave me leave. Tom, at this indulgence, filled a tumbler with brandy, and clasping the black girl in his arms, (as their custom is,) they put both their mouths to the glass, and jointly drank thereout; but unfortunately for Captain Roach, he came into the cabin and detected them in that attitude while drinking; which so provoked him that he ran the end of his cane into Tom's mouth, broke the tumbler, and knocked out all his front teeth. The Captain then ran to his state-room for one of his loaded pistols; but Tom, apprehensive of his danger, jumped overboard. It being dark, and the tide-ebb flowing strong, Tom's canoe dropped astern, took him up, and carried him on shore.

Our Captain was resolved to go on shore to close the breach that was made; but the ship's company all earnestly strove to convince him of the imprudence of going to Tom Ancora's house; yet if he was bent upon going, they entreated him not to eat or drink anything. However, he was resolutely deaf to all their kind expostulations; dressed himself in a scarlet plush suit, put his sword on, and went to Tom's house; but he, being too subtle for the Captain, carried it fair and easy, and seemed to be very friendly, but took care to give the Captain a strong dose of poison, which in three days operated so effectually upon him, that the fingers of both his hands were drawn into the palms, and all his toes were drawn under his feet.

Next morning one Dick Ebrew and his son came on board, and desired to learn what he had eat, whether he was hot or cold, while at Tom Ancora's house; saying, if he would simply tell them, it was not impossible for them to expel the poison and save his life. These two men I have often admired for their meek and loving spirit, far beyond thousands who call themselves Christians. However, all their reasonings to convince him that he was poisoned proved ineffectual; for he insisted he was not; and they as strenuously insisted that he was. At length the benevolent father and his son left the Captain, much grieved that they had not the opportunity of preserving his life; he being a man greatly esteemed among the natives.

When the ship was sailing over the bar, Adam, a negro,

had planned the cutting off the ship's company; which when perceived by the other slaves, they joined the mutiny, and on a sudden rose, and seized the cook, and threw him into the furnace of boiling rice. They likewise attacked the boatswain, took from him his knife, stabbed him in several parts of his body, and threw him overboard. The cooper, hearing the disturbance, came up out of the hold; upon which Adam also seized him; but the cooper said to him, "Adam, you no savee me, *tossae you mini!*" The English of which is, "Don't you know I often give you water?" Adam then said to him, "*Taffue, coopery,*" which is, "Get out of the way." The cooper then got over the quarter-deck bulk-head to the arms-chest, took up a loaded pistol, and shot Adam through the head. The other slaves, at seeing their champion dead, ran all down between decks, and were well secured to prevent another massacre. As the Captain lay dangerously ill, and only five men able to work the ship, we, with the greatest toil, reached the West Indies in three weeks. Upon the ship's arrival there, the owner made the cooper a present of sixty pounds for his services.

While we lay at Calabar, just previous to our sailing, the Captain sent me on shore armed, with two men, to what is called "enforcement of trade." I went on shore with a cutlass, by my side, and in my hands two loaded pistols. When I arrived at the top of the hill I heard an uncommon shrieking of women, and as I drew near some houses, saw a native in a fine silk grass net, so curiously made to fit him, that nothing but his hands and feet appeared; the net ended with a fringe not unlike ruffles. This man is looked upon as both a god and a devil, and all stand in the most profound awe of him, from the highest to the lowest.

I stood still to see the sequel; and observed that in his hand he had a green bough, wherewith he was whipping the women, as they went naked, and chasing them out of one house into another; and as they were exceedingly terrified, and considered it a heavy curse when egbo struck them, they fled from him as we would flee from ten thousand serpents. However, when he had satisfied himself by lashing the poor women, he came out, and through the meshes of his net discovering me, he advanced towards me, with a full purpose to let me also feel the weight of his bough; upon which I instantly drew my hanger, with a resolution to cut off his head. He then ran away, and I saw him no more. Afterwards, I was visited by some of the chief men in the town, saying, "*Bacareau*, you no fear egbo?" I replied, "Not I; and that if he offered to strike me, I would have cut his head off." At which answer they could not help laughing heartily, and then retired.

Chapter Four

I NOW return to continue my account of Captain Roach, and the further particulars of my voyage to Jamaica. My readers may observe, that I left off at the description of our proceedings at Old-Calabar, on our Captain's losing the use of his limbs. He found the poison so to work upon him, that he was unable to help himself. The whole burden then fell on me; nor would he suffer any other to approach him. I conducted myself in this disagreeable function tolerably well, till we anchored under St. Thomas's fort, on a Portuguese island, lying about three hundred miles to the westward of the coast of Africa; where Captain Roach directed me to sell the surplus of cargo, after purchasing the Guinea slaves, &c. I went accordingly on shore with the remaining part of the cargo. The Governor's principal clerk bartered with me for gold-dust, broken and damaged jewels, rings, &c., which amounted to the sum of £630: he put it into a very curiously made bag, the better to enable me to keep it secure. I took it in my right hand, as I was walking down to the beach, swinging it backwards and forwards; a little black boy came behind me, snatched the bag out of my hand, and fled out of sight before I could well look round me. I was in the utmost consternation at so great a loss; but in a few minutes, to my unspeakable satisfaction, I perceived the clerk from whom I had received the gold, hastening down with the bag in his hand, who had met the boy flying up the town with it. He then gave it me, and said, "Sir, be more careful of your property for the future, especially when you are in a strange country." I was inconceivably thankful, and own that this Portuguese was actuated by stronger principles of honour (in this instance to a stranger) than thousands of my country-men would have been to a native of their own country.

By this time our Captain grew worse, and one day with his stool came several large clots of blood, one of which was nearly as large as a pigeon's egg. When I informed him of this, he lifted up his eyes and hands to heaven, repeating these words, "Lord Jesus, receive my spirit." From this time, he voided larger clots of blood; so that it was computed, two or three and thirty pounds of blood had been discharged from him at various times. He charged the surgeon to open him when dead. He soon after made his exit; and upon his body's dissection, the surgeon pointed out to us the cause of his voiding such quantities of blood, which was in consequence of the veins across his stomach being cut by the poison into five hundred pieces. He was then sewed up in his hammock, and committed to the great deep; and I firmly believe had all his sufferings here.

Various occurrences happened in the ship during the Captain's illness: but I shall particularly remark only the circumstances of one, which, I apprehend, was rather of an ominous nature. Every day, in the course of his weakness of body, he made repeated efforts to reach the cabin-windows, in order to receive the cooling air; and at whatever times he looked in the water, a devil-fish was regularly swimming at the stern of the ship: he did not appear to be a fish of prey; but his breadth from fin to fin was about twenty-eight feet, and in length about seven or eight, with a wide tail, and two ivory horns in front. He followed the ship, to our best calculation, near eighteen hundred miles; nor was it remembered by any of the ship's crew that a fish of that nature had made its appearance in the course of any of their voyages. Perpetual attempts to destroy or catch this monster were made, by the fastening a thick rope round the body of a dead negro, and casting him overboard; but it was ineffectual: the fish swam close under our stern, got his horns entangled in the rope, under-run it to the end, and then tossed his refused prey several yards above the water. When the Captain died, he forsook the ship, and we saw him no more.

Our chief Mate, James Seaborn, on the death of Captain Roach, undertook the command of the ship; and after a short passage of a few days she arrived at Jamaica. When the ship sailed from Jamaica, we had a difficult task to steer through the windward passage; but at length we weathered the east end of Jamaica, and directed a steady course between that and Hispaniola, and the east end of Cuba. About three o'clock in the afternoon, having a fair wind, by which the ship was scudding eleven or twelve miles an hour, he suddenly discovered a very large sloop close in shore under Cape-Nichola. Our Captain, being a young mariner, took her to be a New-York sloop, bound for Jamaica. We instantly hauled up our courses, and lay to; but as she swiftly bore down upon us, our Captain shortly found his mistake, as she proved to be a Spanish guarda-la-costa, or, more properly, a Spanish pirate. The enemy's vessel was exceeding large, and full of guns and men: our Captain was then very assiduous, and exerted himself to the utmost in the hopes of saving the ship; but the men would neither fight nor fly; so that he was constrained to surrender the ship, cargo, and men, to the disposal of the enemy.

When we were boarded, the Spanish sailors began to plunder us, stripping and taking all away, from the Captain down to the cabin-boy; nor did they spare the clothes on our backs, but instead of them clothed us with their filthy ragged frocks and drawers. They killed all our poultry, and set us to picking them; put on the ship's large kettle, and boiled both fowls and ducks. They likewise took away all our compasses, save two that had been spoiled with the rain on the coast of Africa. In short, they took away every useful article, and left us totally destitute of carpenters', coopers', and boatswains' tools. They informed us, that, at eight o'clock the next morning, every one of us, without distinction, should be hanged, and that without ceremony. They presented to us the place and the scaffold erected for that purpose, which was on the platform under Cape-Nichola; but the providence of God interposed, by making me the instrument of our deliverance. The circumstance was this:—I frequently kept the ship's accounts in the Captain's absence, and was ordered to do so when he was removed on board the Spanish pirate. I then secured his gold watch, and deposited the same amongst the coals in the fore-peak, and brought our ship to an anchor close under the enemy's stern, where we remained all night.

When the enemy's under-Captain had discontinued his plundering, their principal or Spanish Commander repaired on board the capture, and brought our master with him, in order to spend the evening together; and in the course of their conversation, the Spanish Captain asked Captain Seaborn if he had a watch on board. He replied, "Sir I had a gold watch, and a silver one, but I am afraid they are lost in the plunder." However, the Captain wisely asked me if I knew whether it was stolen, or whether I had taken care of it myself; if I had, he said it would be the means of saving our lives. I told him that I hid it in the fore-peak amongst the coals. I was then directed to go and bring it; but one of the Spanish common seamen, knowing for what I was sent thither, followed me down the fore-scuttle, and when I had pocketed the watch, he took up a billet of wood, struck me a blow on my left ear, which stunned me, and then took the watch out of my pocket. Notwithstanding my insensibility, I could take particular notice of the fellow. In about twenty minutes I came to myself, went and informed our Captain of what had happened, who asked me if I knew the man again. I told him, he was leaning with his left arm on the ship's gunnel: he then informed the Spanish Captain of it, who went with me to the man, and demanded the watch. The fellow went on his knees, and surrendered it, and was afterwards, with all his plundering companions, by the command of their Captain, dismissed from our ship, and sent on board their own. After their Captain had discoursed with ours about the space of forty minutes, he returned on board his own ship likewise.

We still remained in a state of anxiety in respect to our destiny; but at eight o'clock the next morning, the Spanish Captain hailing our ship, desired us to weigh anchor and direct our course for England. The joy which this reprieve produced in our hearts was beyond what I am able to describe. When this ecstacy subsided, we immediately weighed anchor with great pleasure, made sail with a favourable breeze, and in two hours left the land seven leagues astern. But greater misfortunes were yet to come. The third day after our escape from the pirate we apprehended that we were at no great distance from Crooked Island; therefore a diligent look-out at the mast-head was ordered to be kept. Precisely at ten o'clock at night the sentinel called out to the man at the wheel, and begged him instantly to put the helm hard a-lee, as there were fifty sail of ships on the lee-bow at no great distance. We were at that time scudding with the wind quarterly, (all our steering-sails set,) at the rate of twelve or thirteen miles an hour. The ship quickly answered her helm, but having such a crowd of sail upon her, and the mariners not being sufficiently active to haul them down at so short a notice, we found that, instead of shipping, we were surrounded with dreadful breakers on a reef of rocks, and so very steep, that when the ship's stern turned round, any person could have jumped off the ship's tafferel upon them. Having so exceeding swift a way through the water, she drew a little off from the rocks; yet, by reason of her missing stays, she fell off again; and the first blow she struck, a projected part of a rock went through her bottom, and in a few minutes the whole ship was full of water. By the deep sea-line we found that her stern lay in eighty fathoms, and had she not been held fast by this rock, every one on board must inevitably have perished.

In the midst of these suffering seasons, we all experimentally knew the merciful hand of God was over us; for if the ship had not struck on the spot where she did, it would have been impossible for any one on board to have reached the land; as we afterwards found there was no passage through the reef, except that part whereon the vessel was wrecked, Seeing no prospect of ever securing the least part of her hull, we used all diligence, at every opportunity, to save part of her cargo. We speedily hoisted out our long-boat, and stowed several bags of bread therein, together with another fore-sail, wherewith we intended to make a tent on shore; but the boat being exceedingly rotten, with many leaks in her bottom, having no tools on board to stop them, before we could reach the landing-place she sunk to the gunnel, and totally spoiled all our bread; yet, by the assistance of the Almighty, we all escaped to land with the fore-sail, with which, and the help of two long poles, we erected a small tent, to keep off the insufferable heat of the scorching sun.

When the evening approached, the Captain directed us to run the yawl backwards and forwards from the east to the west parts of the island, to discover the town or inhabitants, (if any,) whereby to obtain some refreshments; but, after having spent eight hours in that hazardous excursion, we perceived that the island was totally uninhabited. Here another scene of distress presented itself. As we could get no provision from the ship, we searched the island for both food and water, but without success; nor was the land productive of any animals or vegetables, except an abundance of land-crabs and shell-fish. These marks of desolation and barrenness made us try various resources in order to support life. Accordingly, three or four of us ventured ourselves naked into the sea, to swim on board the ship, if possible, for the purpose of getting such water as was not spoiled; and, notwithstanding the wreck lay full two miles from the shore, yet we effected our purposes in a short time.

Having hoisted out three casks of fresh water, we left them to be driven on shore by the strength of a constant sea-breeze and the waves together, which, in the space of ten minutes, sent them so near the land, as to be rolled up the beach by our seamen on shore. My readers may be surprised at our swimming two miles upon a stretch; but let it be observed, that there were many small rocks lying between the shore and the ship, so that when we were almost wearied out, they served us for resting-places; though we never quitted these rocks, but at the immediate hazard of our lives, seeing there were multitudes of sharks and alligators perpetually sporting throughout the bay.

After we had weathered three weeks in this deplorable situation, exposed to the inclement atmosphere, the mosquitos, like swarms of bees, pierced our flesh severely with their poisonous stings, inasmuch that we were necessitated to bury ourselves in the sand, even our hands and faces, (clearing only our mouths and nostrils at certain times, for the admittance of air,) or we should certainly have been stung to death.

Our Captain then asked who would undertake to proceed with him to the north-west part of the island, as he conceived that would be the only means of finding a remedy. I readily complied with his proposal, and jumped into the boat, accompanied by four others and himself; and, upon our leaving the island, we left those troublesome companions, the insects. Here it may be well to observe the goodness of God in sending these insects to drive us out to sea. Our Captain being inclined to run round the island, in order to make what discoveries we could, he sailed about thirty miles round to the south-west, where we found a fine bay. As we advanced towards the land, we discerned several flamingo birds, a fowl of the first magnitude, which we imagined were some persons who inhabited the place; but when we arrived at the rocks, we found our mistake, and were under the necessity of revisiting that reef of rocks whereon our ship was cast away.

Upon our approach to the shore, several of our people, with joy, desired us to run out to sea, as there was a vessel in the offing. The Captain immediately steered through the gut, and we happily met her about half a mile from the wreck of our ship. When we came near to the stranger, the seamen presented loaded blunderbusses at us, and bade us keep off, or they would certainly fire upon us. We begged to inform them that we were in great distress, our ship being lost on the reef of rocks, and that the remainder of our people were on shore in a tent. Their Captain then, with some warmth, declared, if we did not keep our boat at a greater distance, he would discharge a six-pounder at us, and send both yawl and men to the bottom. He likewise asserted that we were pirates, that our ship was not lost, but riding at anchor; and that we had no authority to lay in those uninhabited parts of the world. We expostulated with him a considerable time, and at length he permitted us to repair on board.

When we had done, the Captain, whose name was Cabel Bean, ran close in shore, embarked the remainder of our distressed companions by the assistance of their yawl, and after having interrogated them respecting their catastrophe, he found that our relation was strictly true.

As we had many valuables on board, which we supposed had received no damage, the vessel (which was called the Potomack sloop) stood off until, with their boats and our yawls, we had saved goods to the amount of one thousand two hundred pounds, in anchors, cables, rigging, rum, pimento, cotton, &c.; and as the vessel had nothing on board but ballast, it was more adapted to receive the spoiled goods. While we were thus employed, a large turtle-boat, from

Virginia, hove in sight; the master's name was Sims, a mulatto; who likewise lent us the assistance of his boat and crew, in recovering the spoils of our cargo. After we had saved everything we could, Sims, the mulatto, took three or four of us, with the two Captains, round to the north side of the island, in order to instruct us in fish-catching, that we might in some degree, alleviate our distresses, if we should at any future period fall into the like situation. Accordingly, we sailed up a salt-water river, where were plenty of mullets, and a young chicken-turtle; and as the water here was amazingly shallow, not more than two feet, we chased those fish backwards and forwards, till we chased them into about six inches water, when falling flat upon our breasts, we caught them without any tackle.

When we repaired to land, with a design to cook our acquisitions, we could neither get fire nor candle; but Mr. Sims produced a tinder-box, and striking fire to the tinder, applied it to some dry grass, and gave it a few shakes in the air, till it was kindled to a fire. We then barbecued the young turtle, and boiled a mullet. Still we were at a loss to obtain fresh water, till Mr. Sims only scratched the sand rather above high-water mark, and, to our astonishment, fresh water sprung up. After we had regaled ourselves, Sims conveyed us in his turtle-boat to the reef of rocks, whereon our ship was cast away. By this time, the seamen of Captain Bean's Potomack had well nigh equipped her, and waited only for the return of their passengers.

When we were all on board, Mr. Sims distributed all the cargo among the sailors belonging to the wreck, and then directed his course towards Boston, in New-England. About three weeks after our departure from the desolate island, early one morning we discovered the Gay-Head of St. Matthias's Vineyard, so called from its appearance in a variety of colours, with a reef of rocks, not more than half a mile astern of us. We came to an anchor about eight o'clock in the evening, with fine pleasant weather; but at ten a tremendous storm arose, which caused the sea to roar dreadfully, and run mountains high.

Precisely at twelve o'clock, as I had the watch upon deck a very heavy sea broke against our bow, which strained the ship exceedingly. I hastily ran to the companion hatchway to call another upon the guard; but suspecting the violent sea to have had a dangerous tendency on the ship, I went immediately to the deep sea-lead, took and hove it over the stern, to judge whether she was riding safe at her anchor or not; but found the lead was under bottom. I ran to the hatchway, called all hands, and informed them the vessel was adrift.

Captain Bean said, in a very solemn manner, "Then the Lord have mercy on our souls: we are every one lost." Immediately the vessel came down with such vehemency upon the rocks, that when the waves returned, they were even up to our gunnel above the water, the sea driving us upon them with such power, that nothing but the omnipotence of God could have preserved us from the imminent danger. The sea still followed us like rolling mountains, even to the beach, and dashed the sloop so violently against the rocks that we entertained no other idea but that she would be broken in a thousand pieces. In this situation I pulled off my frock and drawers, which was all the Spaniards had left me, when the next wave washed them overboard, and left me completely destitute of clothing of any kind; nor was it in the power of any person on board to afford me any relief. However, I proposed to three more on board, that could swim tolerably well, to plunge ourselves overboard, and attempt to gain the shore; persuaded that, if this plan could be effected, a method might be taken to save the lives of those on board, who otherwise must have been drowned. Accordingly four of us cast ourselves overboard, and endeavoured to swim on shore; but in the attempt we were carried backwards out of our depth by a raging surf; nor could we get firm footing on the sandy beach till the wave had spent itself.

At length, after having our bodies dangerously hurt, and

driven about by every succeeding wave, we got safe on shore, and hailed the others on board the wreck to send a rope on shore, in order to haul them, one by one, to land. They did so, and we rescued all our poor distressed companions from the remorseless deep. After this they unanimously consented to travel a little way into the country, and almost compelled me to go with them, naked as I was ; but I declined it, owing to shame and confusion ; and while the others were ransacking the island in quest of provision, &c., I was solitarily bewailing my deplorable and hapless state between two small rocks, almost starved with hunger and cold. At seven o'clock in the evening, it being dusk, one of our men came running towards me, and compelled me to go to a tavern with him, which was at the distance of seven miles. I asked him if he had brought me any thing to cover me. He replied, "No ;" but that there was speedy help for me. I readily complied, and with much difficulty reached the tavern at midnight. The messenger went in, and informed the host of my case, who brought me out a pair of red breeches, which was all he had left after supplying the rest.

Ebenezer Allen, Governor of the island, and who dwelt about six miles from the tavern, hearing of our distress, made all possible haste to relieve us ; and when he arrived at the tavern, (accompanied by his eldest sons,) he took Captain Seaborn, his black servant, Joseph, and myself, and escorted us to his own house. Between eleven and twelve at night we reached the Governor's mansion. Being ashamed to be seen, we would fain have hid ourselves in any dark hole, as it was a truly magnificent building : but, to our astonishment, we were received into the great parlour, where were sitting, by the fire-side, two fine ladies attending the spit, on which was a heavy quarter of house-lamb.

Observing a large mahogany table, spread with a fine damask cloth, and every knife, fork, and plate laid in a genteel manner, I thought it was intended for some persons of distinction, or, at least, for the family supper. In a short time the meat was laid on the table, yet nobody sat down to eat; and as we were almost hid in one corner of the room, the ladies turned round and said, "Poor men, why do you not come to supper?" I replied, "Madam, we had no idea that it was prepared for us." The ladies then entreated us to eat without any kind of fear of them, assuring us that it was prepared for none others; and none of us having eaten any thing for near five-and-thirty hours before, we picked the bones of the whole quarter; to which we had plenty of rich good cider to drink. After supper we went to bed, and enjoyed so profound a sleep, that the next morning it was difficult for the old gentleman to awake us.

The following day I became a partaker of several garments; and as I was happily possessed of a little learning, it caused me to be more abundantly caressed by the whole family. This unexpected change of circumstance and diet I experienced in a very uncommon manner; but as I was strictly trained up a Churchman, and could not support the idea of a Dissenter, (although, God knows, I had well nigh by this time dissented from all that was truly good,) this proved a bar to my promotion; and my strong propensity to sail for England, to see my mother, prevented my acceptance of the greatest offer I ever received in my life. For, when the day came that we were to quit the island, and cross the Sound, over to a town called Sandwich, (on the continent,) the young squire took me apart, and entreated me to stay with them; saying, that if I would, nothing should be lacking to render my situation agreeable.

As there were very few white men on the island, I was fixed upon, (if willing,) to espouse one of the Governor's daughters. I have been informed that he was immensely rich, having on the island two thousand head of cattle, and twenty thousand sheep, and every acre of land thereon belonging to himself. However, I could not be prevailed upon to accept the offer; therefore the Governor furnished us with forty shillings each, and gave us a pass over to the town of Sandwich. Upon our arrival there we waited upon Mr. Silas Bourn, Justice of the Peace, who treated us courteously, ordered us to sign our names to a certain paper, which he sent to the keeper of a tavern, whereby we could have every thing we wished for.

After taking our leave of Justice Bourn, we set out for Plymouth, which, we were informed, was the first spot whereon the Americans landed when they first went over to inhabit that part of the world. It appeared a low, mean place, with only a small spired meeting-house, which they built before they had raised one dwelling-house: such was their zeal for the glory of God! We passed through this tract of land without a main road to guide us, till we came to a wood. The woods in this part of the world are variegated with numberless rows of tall pines, which naturally grow at a tolerable distance from one another, so that they resemble a gentleman's park, and form a beautiful appearance. We continued travelling till it began to grow dark; and finding no house in our way since we left Plymouth, we concluded that we must pitch our tent in the woods all night. However, at about seven o'clock we came to a small public-house. After we had supped, I craved the hospitality of an old Englishman in providing a bed for each of us; but he very roughly refused, seeing we were entire strangers.

As we were about to continue our nocturnal journey, a poor woman ran up to us, and insisted upon our returning to her house, where we should be hospitably accommodated with every thing we wanted for that night. This being the 1st of November, and the winter there just set in, we were, whilst by the fire, almost burned on one side, but nearly frozen on the other. As soon as daylight appeared we arose, and took our leave of the old woman, after returning her many thanks. At half-past eleven we reached the beautiful town of Hanover. Here the buildings were all truly magnificent. The inhabitants, were polite, wealthy, and of an agreeable mien.

At the north-west part of the town was a very fine road, which extended itself to the sea shore. In the centre of this road stands a stately church, conveniently situated for travellers, who frequently have recourse thereto, in their journeys on Sabbath-days. One Sunday, as my companions and I were crossing the church-yard, at the time of divine service, a well dressed gentleman came out of the church, and said, "Gentlemen, we do not suffer any person in this country to travel on the Lord's day." We gave him to understand that it was necessity which constrained us to walk that way, as we were all ship-wrecked at St. Martin's Vineyard, and were travelling to Boston. The gentleman was still dissatisfied, but quitted our company, and went into the church. When we had gone a little farther, a large white house caught our attention. The door being wide open, we reasonably imagined it was not without servants or others; but as we went into the kitchen, nobody appeared to be within, either above or below. However, I advised my companions to stay in the house until some person should arrive. They did so, and in a short time two ladies richly dressed, with a footman following them, came in through the kitchen; and, notwithstanding they turned round and saw us, (who in so dirty and disagreeable a garb might have terrified them exceedingly,) yet neither of them took any notice of us, nor did they demand our reason for such an intrusion.

About a quarter of an hour afterwards, a footman entered the kitchen with the cloth, and a large two-quart silver tankard full of rich cider, also a loaf and cheese; but we, did not attempt to partake of it. At length the ladies coming into the kitchen, and viewing us in our former position, asked why we did not refresh ourselves with what was set before us? Upon which I urged the others to join with me in the acceptance of so hospitable a proposal. After this the ladies made a familiar inquiry into our situation. I gave them as particular an account of every occurrence as I could.

We then asked the ladies if they could furnish us with a lodging that evening. They replied, if we proceeded farther, we should doubtless be entertained by their brother, a Quaker, about seven miles farther off. We thanked them, and set forward, and at about eight o'clock arrived at their brother's house. Fatigued with our journey, we hastened into the parlour, and delivered our message: whereupon a gentleman quickly gave us to understand that he was the Quaker referred to by the ladies, who (total strangers as we were) used us with a degree of hospitality impossible to be exceeded.

After our banquet, the gentleman took us up into a spacious bed-chamber, with desirable bedding, and very costly chintz curtains. We enjoyed a sound night's rest, arose between seven and eight the next morning, and were entertained with a good breakfast. We returned many thanks for his friendship and liberality, and departed for Boston. Here all the land was strewed with plenty; and their orchards were filled with apple and pear trees. They had cider-presses in the centre of their orchards, and great quantities of neat cider of which any person might become a partaker for the mere trouble of asking. We soon entered Boston, a commodious and beautiful city, where I resided four months.

Nothing was wanting during our continuance here: affluence flowed in upon the inhabitants from all parts of the continent. I never remember to have heard one oath uttered, or the name of God mentioned, save upon a religious occasion, during the four months I tarried at that place; nor is there one lewd house suffered in the whole town, or any Sabbath-breaking. It was a pleasure to buy and sell among them, because I never found an individual guilty of extortion. Would to God I could say this of the inhabitants of Great Britain!

Chapter Five

ON our arrival at Boston we applied for the salvage of our goods which were saved out of the ship Scipio; but Captain Clark refused to make us any satisfaction, as his vessel was wrecked by waiting to take us up. Upon this, a certain gentleman of that city undertook our cause, and commenced an action against Captain Clark in the Admiralty-court. The defendant stood the trial before Judge Byfield; and after a hearing of about an hour, the Judge addressed Captain Clark, and asked him if he thought we had not suffered sufficiently already? He therefore said, "As you saved the cargo of your own vessel, I hereby decree that they shall all receive double salvage." Then Captain Clark, though deemed by the inhabitants a covetous man, told the Judge, cheerfully, that it should be so; and that he would moreover make each of us a present of ten pounds currency, exclusive of our respective salvage. Thus ended our law-suit, and we had a sufficiency to fit us out with every necessary article for sea again.

I embraced the first opportunity of sailing for Antigua, in the West Indies, where I got my discharge; and having a strong inclination to return to my native country, I entered into an agreement with Captain Skutt, then lying in the harbour of St. John's, the principal town of Antigua. While we were waiting here for a freight for England, there came on a very terrible hurricane, which drove us out of the harbour into the offing; yet we providentially sustained little damage; and reached in the space of eight days, the harbour of St. John's again. When we had taken in part of our home-ward-bound merchandise, the ship was ordered to the island of Montserrat, about ten leagues to leeward of Antigua, there to procure the residue of our cargo.

This island chiefly consists of numerous lofty and barren mountains, with an unnavigable harbour, rendered so by a multiplicity of small sharp-pointed rocks, several of which at ebb-tide are one, two, or more feet above water. There is likewise a very mean and inconsiderable town, which has little or no correspondence with others in the adjacent islands. The name of this town is Basseterre, and is situated in view of the islands of Nevis, St. Christopher, and Guadaloupe. Here we were necessitated to travel seven or eight miles over rocks, and through many valleys, to get fire-wood, of a tree called manchineel. It is one of the most beautiful trees, probably, in the known world; and bears an apple, the odour whereof is not unlike that of our English golden rennets, and of an equal form and size; but every part of it is one of the rankest poisons,—root, stem, branches, leaves, and fruit. When I first went to Jamaica, I saw one of those trees, which was full of fruit, and spread its branches and leaves as wide as our great walnut-trees in England. I simply knocked down one of the apples, and, ignorant of the consequence, was going to eat it (as it was pleasing to the eye,) when a black man, observing me, ran with uncommon swiftness, and snatched it from my hand; giving me to understand, that if I had eaten it, all my teeth would have fallen out of my head. He told me also that if any person was to stand under that tree in a shower of rain, the drops falling from it on any part of the skin, would take it off. As our men were cutting those trees for fire-wood at

Montserrat, they had their eyes closed and swelled in such a manner, that we were apprehensive they never could recover their sight; but they recovered in a short time.

When the ship was ready for sailing, we weighed anchor, and sailed for Bristol, where we arrived after seven weeks' passage. After a few weeks, I shipped myself with Captain James Seaborn in a second voyage, for Old Calabar, on the coast of Africa. Here I was made gunner of the ship; and soon after was ordered for South Carolina. Thence we steered our course, with a delightful gale, to the Bristol Channel. On coming to England, I repaired to Bristol, and from thence set off for London, to visit my mother, whom I had not seen for ten years past. My family being in low circumstances, I was obliged to go again to sea; and the first trip was in a coasting sloop to Wisbeach, with Captain John Heath. When I returned, I shipped myself with Captain Thomas Long, for Antigua. When I had made this voyage, I agreed with Captain Rogers for a voyage up the Mediterranean.

We sailed from the Downs in the month of January, 1733, after riding out many vehement storms in that sea. The whole fleet sailed down the Channel with very promising weather; but before we made any progress, the wind suddenly varied, and blew with such violence that the greater part of the fleet were scattered, and their sails torn to atoms; therefore such as could, returned to Spithead, while the others were dispersed abroad, and driven to the coast of France. But our Captain, being an obstinate, though an experienced, seaman, was determined to proceed. The consequence was, we were bearing to windward for full five weeks incessantly under reefed courses, the sea making continual breaches over the ship. We did not, during that time, dress any provisions; neither had any of us a dry thread upon our backs.

One night, in particular, the wind, being at north-west, attacked us so violently, that the ship was laid hatches under water, and the forescuttle, where we came up, being unfortunately open, every sea poured itself down into the hold, insomuch that the ship was sunk very near two streaks in the water. The Captain was at the same time cursing, swearing, and roaring, like an infernal spirit; and had it not been for the alacrity of one of our seamen, who ran up the weather-main-shrouds, and conveyed himself under water to come at the lee-main-sheet, and let it go (which, as the main-sail was set, naturally pressed the ship down to leeward,) we must inevitably have foundered. When the main-sheet was let fly, the main-sail went all to shivers; the fore-sail then wore the ship round, and brought her starboard side to the wind, which blew her upon an even keel. She lay for a long time like a log upon the waves, and having five feet water in her hold. We had recourse to both pumps, and in about five hours cleared her, and proceeded on our voyage; but the obstinacy of the Captain occasioned the loss of the whole cargo, and this considerable loss fell upon the consigners. As our first port of delivery was Marseilles, in the south of France, down to the Gulf of Lyons, in the Straits of Gibraltar, we went thither, and offered to the consignees their cargo; but they refused to accept it. This obliged us to carry it to Genoa, where it was likewise refused. From hence we steered up to Leghorn, and this being the last port of delivery, the freighter's correspondents were obliged to accept it, good or bad, agreeable to charter. When our cargo was discharged, and our ship re-laden we departed.

After we had been to Marseilles, Genoa, and Leghorn, we sailed for England. When we arrived off the Isle of Wight, a tender, which lay in the Channel, pressed our whole ship's crew. After having been on board the tender upwards of a week, one part of us were sent on board the Lenox, of seventy guns, and the other on board the Ipswich, of the same force. After lying at Spithead ten months, under an arbitrary Lieutenant, I was removed on board the Phœnix, Captain Trivil Caley, who was a gentleman and a Christian. He encouraged religious discipline on board; nor did he ever neglect to order his Chaplain to attend his invalids, at five o'clock in the morning, both at Portsmouth and at Gosport, and would constantly visit every patient respectively, on his knees, at their bed-sides, with all the devotion becoming a Christian. Never was a Commander so caressed by a ship's company as Captain Caley, and his men were equally dear to him. So entirely cautious was he before he spoke to any man on board, from the highest to the lowest, that he even drew the attention of strangers. For my part, I could never look at him but with uncommon satisfaction. Happy, truly happy, it proved for me that I fell in with so worthy a Christian; otherwise, what with the hell of uncommon curses and oaths, accompanied by an habitual course of cruel behaviour on the part of two Lieutenants, I must have died under my burden.

At that time I was grievously opposed with the rheumatism. However, early one morning, God undertook my cause, and I began thus to reason with myself: "The rheumatism! What is it?" And it was strongly suggested to me, "It is a violent cold." I then asked, "What is most proper as a remedy for the cold?" and was answered, "Spring water." On this I called a man, whose name was Tom Lewis, and requested him to procure me five or six shirts, and air them well. I desired him also to fill a large pitcher of water, and bring it instantly to me, and I would drink till I could drink no more. He endeavoured to dissuade me, assuring me that it would kill me. "Notwithstanding," added he, "if you are bent upon taking it, I will get it quickly." He did so; and when I had drank freely, I laid down on the bed, and Tom covered me up very warm. After I had laid about the space of half an hour, I put my head under the clothes, and breathed hard on the pit of my stomach: this produced a profuse perspiration.

I then desired my attendant to bring me half-a-dozen warm flannels, in order to rub me from head to foot: he did this likewise, and continued running till I made five shirts quite wet. When I had put on the sixth shirt, I told Thomas, that I was totally exempt from every symptom of the rheumatism. I then jumped out of bed, dressed myself, and asked what was for dinner? He replied, "Salt fish and potatoes." And although I had not enjoyed one meal for eight or ten weeks before, yet I went down, and made as hearty a meal as ever I did in my life, and then walked a mile on shore, by way of recreation. Here I considered that nothing was impossible to Him who had all power in heaven and in earth. Two or three days after this I was pronounced "able," and went on board the Lenox, the ship I formerly belonged to.

On Christmas-eve, in the year 1734, I espoused Mary Verney, in the twenty-second year of her age; at which time I was in my twenty-third year. After remaining on board the ship for two months, orders were sent down to Sir John Norris, on board the Britannia, a first-rate of 100 guns; the Barfleur, Admiral Balchan, of 90 guns; and the Lancaster, of 80 guns, Admiral Haddock, together with twenty-five sail of the line, to sail immediately for Lisbon, to protect the King of Portugal's Brazil fleet from the threats of the Spaniards. Here myself, with several others, were turned over from the Lennox on board the Grafton, of 70 guns, and sailed in company with the fleet, for Lisbon, and arrived in the Tagus some time in the month of May, 1735, where we lay ten months at anchor, in which time the Brazil fleet arrived, and orders were sent from England for Admiral Haddock's squadron to return thither.

Previous to our departure from Lisbon, the King of Portugal, with his brother, the black Prince, came on board the three Admirals, whose ships were dressed in various colours, and made a very brilliant appearance, His Portuguese Majesty allowed every man and boy in the fleet one pint of wine per day, with fresh provisions every day till the completion of our voyage.

We sailed for England in the beginning of January, 1736, and arrived off the rocks of Scilly the latter end of the same month, where our ship was well nigh lost; it being indispensably necessary for us to beat to windward under reefed courses; but, thank God, we were preserved in this storm also, and arrived safe in Chatham river, where we were paid off, February 6, 1736. I then came directly to London; nor have I ever been to sea since.

I now entered upon a new scene of life; for although I had been brought up to the sea, and had no friends to supply my necessities at home, yet I was resolved, through the help of the Almighty, to have recourse to any employment rather than abide in the state of life I formerly did; a life attended with all manner of sufferings, and wickedness in the highest degree. Indeed, God never left me without conviction, which constantly rendered my mind unhappy; and my conscience up-braided me for the commission of sin.

Chapter Six

BEING now in a married state, and desirous to lead a regular life, I habituated myself to the Church service; but finding the Churchmen living as did other people, and having no Christian friend to converse with, I knew not what step to take, and therefore readily concluded religion was a mere farce. At the same time, being subject to the weight of many temporal distresses, it pleased God to point me out, in a few months, a school at Staplefoot-Tauney, near Passingford-Bridge, in the county of Essex, erected by a Lady Luther, who spared no pains in its building; and also bestowed many donations towards the support and maintenance thereof. My whole salary amounted to fourteen pounds per annum; ten pounds whereof was the salary from the school; two pounds from Lady Luther, and the like sum from Mr. Moot, a wealthy farmer; with as many day-scholars as I could get on my own account. I soon raised a considerable school, and sent to London for my wife, and all my goods. The lady invited me three days in the week, with the Curate of the parish, to dine with her; and every other day, if I thought proper, to accompany her servants at their dinner in Knaves-Hall, as they termed it. I now began to be much delighted with my situation, and spared no diligence to bring the children forward in their learning; and indeed the success I met with caused the school to be recommended throughout the country.

The Curate of the parish frequently called upon me, decoyed me to his lodgings, about three miles from the school, to join him in smoking and drinking. He also pressed me to sing him a sea-song; and I was generally detained so very late at night, that I could scarcely find my way home. Once, as the Curate and myself were going from Lady Luther's over the fields to my school, I took the liberty to quote some passages of Scripture, relating to our immoral proceedings. My guide laughed heartily, and said, "Told, are you so great a blockhead as to believe the Scripture? It is nothing but a pack of false stuff." This surprised me much, and from that time I separated myself from his company; and God, in His providence, disunited me from those dead Christians, by the following simple circumstance.

The wood I had bespoke for firing not coming in so soon as I expected, I acquainted farmer Mills, on the opposite side of the church-yard, who gave me leave to send my boys into his field, where they might collect a quantity sufficient for my use until the bespoke fire-wood came in; and seeing it was on the farmer's own ground, I had no conception of any impropriety; yet this, through the complaint of an old woman, (who before expressed the sincerest regard for myself and wife,) proved the cause of my removal out of the country.

Sir Edward Smith, then lord of the manor, sent for Lady Luther, and desired to know what kind of a school-master she had brought into the country, and whether he ever taught his children their catechism. She answered, that I bore the best of characters, and had brought the children forward in their education in an extraordinary manner, and that I taught the children their catechism every Thursday. Sir Edward then asked how I came to leave out the eighth commandment: therefore insisted upon my dismission from the school, and departed from the town immediately. He would not hear the circumstance face to face; so I was under the necessity of hiring a waggon to carry all my goods back to London; and was at a loss what method to pursue for the maintenance of my family; but in a short time a clerk's place offered at King's Wharf, to a dealer in coals and timber. I remained there about four months, when my mistress leaving off business, I was necessarily discharged, and was left destitute of employment for some time; nor could I obtain any relief, or procure the least employ. I therefore resolved to submit to any office to procure a subsistence; and accordingly engaged myself to a bricklayer in Watling-Street, to keep his books, and at vacant opportunities to attend the labourers. Here I continued six or seven years, and afterwards served Mr. John Pankeman.

In the course of my services with him, a young man, who was a bricklayer, came and asked me, if I could help him to business. I answered him roughly; which he received with great meekness: this struck me with surprise. I then called him back and desired him to wait on a certain master bricklayer the next morning, who, I believed, could find him employment. He went accordingly, and the gentleman admitted him into his service. This young man was a happy instrument of leading me out of darkness into God's marvellous light.

Here my readers will permit me to revert to my earliest days; and, as I have already set forth the manner of God's working upon my soul, to the time of my admission into Edward Colson's Hospital, I shall occasionally recur to some things of a spiritual nature, which I experienced there.

When I first was admitted into that school, the parting with my tenderhearted nurse brought me under much distress of mind; yet I constantly found the Spirit of God working powerfully upon me; nor could I ever find peace but when meditating on things divine. My thoughts, when at prayers in the school three times every day, were carried up into heaven with the most solemn ardent desire; and when we assembled in the College-church, which we regularly did every Sabbath-day, the service there was to me a heaven upon earth. Here I drank deep into the bliss of the ever-blessed and adorable Jesus, till I arrived at the age of ten years; by which time I had made some proficiency in learning, and was approved of by the Minister, who came twice a week to instruct us in religious principles; so that, in a short time, I was entitled a monitor.

I then began to read pious books, especially the Pilgrim's Progress. This set me on fire for God and heavenly bliss, and wrought in me the utmost horror of taking the Lord's name in vain, or of telling a lie; and as there were a few lads in the same order as myself that were piously inclined, so we often read the Pilgrim's Progress together. One Lord's Day, in particular, being at the College-church, the Rev. Mr. Sutton preached a very alarming discourse upon the things of eternity, to a crowded congregation. The fashion was then for the women to go naked breasted; nor was there a woman to be found in the College but appeared in this indecent manner: yet the discourse, in a great measure, effected its design; nor do I remember to have seen anything of that kind in Bristol afterwards. Many of our boys were deeply affected by the sermon, so that when we came home, several of us entered into an agreement to pinch the tongue of him that told a lie, or mentioned the Lord's name in an irreverent way.

When I was about twelve years of age, I was more acquainted with divine things, but not with myself as a sinner. Sitting one day, reading the Pilgrim's Progress, I suddenly laid down the book, leaned my right elbow on my knee, with my hand supporting my head, and meditated in the most solemn manner upon the awfulness of eternity. Suddenly I was struck as with a hand on the top of my head, which affected my whole frame; the blow was immediately followed by a voice, with these words, "Dark! dark! dark!" and although it alarmed me prodigiously, yet upon the recovery from so sudden a motion, I found myself broad awake in the world of sin. Notwithstanding all my former happiness, I now found nothing could give me satisfaction; nor could I ever rest satisfied about my salvation, as temptations from the world, the flesh, and the devil were ever besetting me.

One day, the boys being permitted to go to visit their friends, I obtained permission likewise, although I had no relation or friend in the city; my mother and two sisters residing in London, and my two elder brothers residing in the country. However, several of the boys accompanied me that afternoon to a river, called Broad Stony, near the city, for the purpose of learning to swim: and as I was strongly desirous of learning that art, several of the smaller boys, with myself, went into the pond, adjoining to that river. I ventured beyond the others; but, in attempting to swim, struck out of my depth, and was, for some time, struggling for life. My companions, who sat upon the bank on the other side of the river, imagined I was taking my pastime, by reason of my rising above water and diving again, and had no conceptions that I was on the verge of being drowned, till they perceived that I sunk, and they could see me no more. At this they were in the utmost consternation, not knowing what to do; but seeing some hay-makers at the farther end of the meadow, they ran with all possible haste, and informed them that a boy was drowned. Providentially there was a Dutchman among the hay-makers, who, upon hearing the news, threw down his hay-fork, ran to the river-side, inquired where I was perceived to sink, and jumped in without pulling off any of his clothes. He groped about for a considerable time, but I could not be found, as I had shot a great distance from the spot where the children perceived me to sink. I was now given up for lost; but as the Dutchman was swimming to the bank where a willow-bush grew out at the side, in order to haul himself out of the pond, he felt about with one of his legs just before he came to the bank; and, as my head was covered with mud, with my heels upright, he providentially struck his foot against mine, and joyfully gave the signal that I was found. He went down, brought me up, and landed me on the bank; but not the least signs of life were discernible in me. He held me with my heels upwards for some minutes, and then concluded my life was gone; yet it came into his mind to try another method. Accordingly he swam across the river, and went a little way up the hill, where there was a small alehouse. He got from thence a quartern of brandy, and swam over the river back again into the meadow, holding up the brandy, in one hand, and swimming with the other. My jaws were firmly set together, nor was there any motion of breath to be perceived; yet he put some brandy into his mouth, forced my jaws open, and blew repeatedly half a quartern of spirits down my throat. He also blew some up my nostrils, and into my ears; and in about three quarters of an hour my left eye flew open, and I gave a great loud shriek. They then carried me to Baptist-Mills, where in about four hours I recovered my senses, so as to have a faint knowledge of one or two of the boys.

I was then conveyed home to the school, but with an excruciating pain, equal to the being cut through in the middle of my body; nor did I enjoy an exemption therefrom for several years together; neither do I remember a single twelvemonth, for a dozen years successively, but this pain produced two, three, or more fits of sickness every year; and many of them brought me near the grave. When I went to school, Mr. Samuel Gardiner, the principal master of the Hospital, having been informed of the circumstance, punished me severely, as a strict charge had been delivered by him that none of us should go near the water, one of his scholars having been drowned some time before.

I hope my readers will suspend their judgment, in censuring what I am now about to relate, although it may appear rather incredible. The circumstance was this: although I was deprived of my natural senses, and had no ideas of the things of this world, yet my spirit was permitted by God, both to behold and experience that which I believe few in the body ever did. My entrance into this blissful vision, as it appeared to me, was, that I emerged out of thick darkness into a most glorious city; the lustre of which as far outshone the brightness of the noon-day sun, as that brightness transcends the rays of the moon. This empyreal light shone with a resplendent power on the city, and illuminated even the darkness through which I seemed to urge my way, and enforce my entrance into that beatific state; and although we cannot retain a steadfast eye upon the sun, when in its meridian splendour, yet I found no impediment to my sight in looking with a rapturous ardency on this heavenly scene, the beams whereof darted from the south-east, with a refulgence above the highest conception. There was also some resemblance of a bottom, or floor, not unlike glass; but neither the city nor bottom were of any substance. The inhabitants were all in the form of men, arrayed in robes of the finest quality, from their necks down to their feet; yet they also appeared to me of no substance. What particularly took my attention was, that not one of these celestial bodies was under any degree of labour to walk, as they all glided swiftly along, as if carried by the wind. This was my own case, clothed in the finest of linen, and conveyed with the like celerity. No speech or language was needful there, as they were all one soul. The solemn, sacred joy, and uninterrupted peace I then possessed, all language fails me to point out. I had no imagination of evil, or any temptation thereto, but was completely happy.

Another point of this vision I would remark, before I close the subject, is, while those blessed spirits were performing their aerial course, one of them, at a small distance on my right hand, turned round and looked steadfastly at my raiment; and the glory that beamed from his countenance united us together as one. O! who can express the sweet, pleasant, and serene tranquillity I then enjoyed; but, on a sudden, I lost all sense of this very desirable state, and sensibly apprehended my being brought again into a sinful world; the coming into which was as through a sea of blood and fire. This was the sequel and conclusion of that awful dispensation of the righteous God to me, well knowing how He had disposed of me for many years past, that I might be made perfect through sufferings, and drink deep into His cup, and be baptized with His baptism.

Since the time I was particularly convinced of sin, by reading the Pilgrim's Progress, the Spirit of God never left me without conviction; nor do I remember ever to have fallen into any outward sin but I reflected upon it with abhorrence, and was also often terrified with awful dreams. When on my first passage to Jamaica, I was grievously exercised in mind, as not one of the mariners had the least concern for God or the salvation of their souls, but, on the contrary, appeared to be greedy of eternal death and damnation. And, as St. Paul saith, "Evil communications corrupt good manners," so they not only corrupted my manners, but my morals also. I, being unacquainted with the devices of the devil, began to doubt whether all those persons who seemed happy in themselves, could be lost eternally, although they lived such horrid lives.

When we arrived at Jamaica, I found the inhabitants corresponded with those reasonings; nor do I remember to have met with one man or woman who had the fear of God before their eyes in the town of Kingston, or Port-Royal, or even the form of godliness. They were much addicted to cursing, swearing, whoredom, lying and Sabbath-breaking; exercising the utmost cruelty on their unhappy negro slaves without remorse. When I went on shore at the east end of Kingston, I saw a stout black man, about thirty-six years of age, brought down to the crane, by his master, and for the commission of some little error, delivered up to be punished.

The mode of punishment was as follows:—The boatswain tied both wrists together with a strong cord; then hooked the crane between his wrists, and hoisted his body nearly a foot from the floor. Then he took a whip, composed of cow's-skin, which, when dried hard and twisted lengthways, forms a kind of screw, the outward edge of which is extremely sharp. A negro, in obedience to the boatswain's commands, began the direful action, in the presence of his vile master, accompanied by two others of the same complexion, gazing upon the pitiable object with delight. After the executioner, with one hundred lashes, had reduced his body from neck to ankles into one wound, and human nature was no longer able to support itself under the stroke, the poor man hung down his head, and received the remaining cuts like a stock or a stone, faintly uttering, "O me deady, me deady!" Nor did this move the accursed fiend, his master, till the poor tortured object appeared in his last gasps. He then desired the boatswain's mate to desist for a few moments, and approached the almost expiring slave; when taking a more particular survey of his wounds from head to foot, and perceiving two or three spaces which had not been laid open, he instantly ran to the boatswain's mate, and compelled him to lash him there also, and make him all alike. When this was done he was loosed; and, having no strength to stand, he lay as dead, while he was washed from head to foot in a tub of salt-beef pickle, placed on the wharf for that purpose. I was astonished that the excruciating pains produced by the pickle did not put a speedy end to his existence. The heathen (his master) tarried to behold this operation also, and afterwards walked off, well satisfied.

This deed was not executed in a corner, or done privily, but upon the open wharf, and in a nominal Christian Protestant country; but if the word "Christian" implies, (which it unquestionably doth,) one who has the mind of Christ, then there can be no breach of charity in pronouncing such wretches as these, children of the devil, rather than the children of God. This horrid barbarity overspread the island of Jamaica in the year 1727, and I fear the same spirit still prevails there. Our fellow-creatures are clandestinely taken away from their native country, utterly against the consent of their parents and themselves, and kept in slavery to the latest moment of their lives, with their children, and their children's children, unto many generations.

I can never sufficiently praise the Almighty for my happy deliverance from the slave-trade, seeing it is one of the basest practices under the sun. Surely an immediate curse from God attends upon it, as few voyages are made to those parts in which the crews are not thinned by poison, suicide, ill usage, and every species of destruction. God followed me with daily convictions of sin; yet, having an evil precedent always before me, and the corruptions of my own nature incessantly prompting me to sin, I sometimes gave way thereto against the light of conscience, knowing but very little of the corrupt fountain from whence those currents flowed. I found that, when the bank was broken, the breach was made wider and wider; and being at that time between seventeen and eighteen years of age, my carnal passions getting the dominion over me, I was oftentimes overcome with swearing, drunkenness, and lewdness, as also divers other evils: therefore, what with my terrified conscience, and disappointments in temporals, my life became completely miserable; and, for about ten years, I continued in that unsettled state, sinning and repenting; yet I never was without fear of death, hell, and judgment.

Chapter Seven

IN July, 1740, Mr. Charles Casper Greaves, the young bricklayer already spoken of, introduced me among the people called Methodists. I observed something in the countenance and behaviour of this young man, very different to what I beheld in others, as well as myself; yet I treated him with ridicule and contempt; and sometimes cursed and swore at him, and told him his whole fraternity was a mixture of false prophets and hypocrites: all which he bore with unwearied patience, without returning me one evil word or look. His countenance appeared full of holy grief; which greatly condemned me, although I concealed it from him. At twelve o'clock he asked me where I dined. I answered him very roughly, "In the hay-loft." He then said, "I will go with you." So we ascended together, and as soon as we were seated on the trusses of hay, he took a Prayer-book out of his pocket, and read a few verses out of the Psalms, and asked me what I thought of those words. As I was fond of the Scriptures, I was the more confounded, well knowing they condemned me. When he perceived me silent, he asked me to go with him that evening to hear the Rev. Mr. Wesley at the Foundery. I begged him, for God's sake, never to ask me questions of that kind any more, for I was determined never to go thither; and said, if my wife should come to know it, she would never forgive me. He said no more; but in that instant, God began to work powerfully upon my soul. Then the eye of my mind saw the Son of God sitting on His throne to judge the world, and such peace resting upon me as tongue cannot express. I found my spirit now much united to Mr. Greaves, and therefore related my experience to him. I then proposed going with him to hear the Rev. Mr. Wesley; and accordingly we repaired to the Foundery, but were disappointed.

The next morning he took me to Short's-gardens, to hear Mr. Wesley; but we were disappointed there likewise. He then said I might depend upon hearing Mr. Wesley next Sunday morning, at five o'clock. I answered him roughly, and told him he might call on me if he thought proper; and gave him directions where I lived. He was at my house precisely at four o'clock in the morning, and I went with him to the Foundery. As we were passing through Cheapside, he asked me if I had an idea of what was become of all those who walked that street fourscore or a hundred years ago? This prepared my mind for hearing the word; and, as God had already wrought graciously on my soul, I was the better prepared to receive instructions. When we entered the Foundery, I gazed about me to make observations. Finding it a ruinous place, with an old pantile covering, a few rough deal boards put together to constitute a temporary pulpit, and several other decayed timbers, which composed the whole structure, I began to think it answered the description given of it. In one corner sat three or four old women, one of whom appeared like a statue, with her apron over her face, nor was she uncovered during the whole service. The enemy of souls immediately suggested that she was an hypocrite. My friend, Mr. Greaves, stood close behind, to prevent my going out, to which I was strongly tempted; and had it not been for the multitude of people assembled together, and the profound seriousness which appeared in the countenance of every person, I should have given way to the temptation, and thereby have lost the greatest blessing I ever experienced.

Exactly at five o'clock a whisper ran through the congregation, "Here he comes! here he comes!" I had a curiosity to see his person, which, when I beheld, I much despised. The enemy of souls suggested, that he was some farmer's son, who, not able to support himself, was making a penny in this low manner. He passed through the congregation into the pulpit, and, having his robes on, I expected he would have begun with the Church service; but, to my astonishment, he began with singing a hymn, with which I was almost enraptured; but his extempore prayer was quite unpleasant, as I thought it favoured too much of the Dissenter. After this, he took his text in the second chapter of the first Epistle general of St. John, 12, 13, "I write unto you, little children, because your sins are forgiven you," &c. The enemy now suggested that he was a Papist, as he dwelt so much on forgiveness of sins. Although I had read this portion of Scripture many times before, yet I never understood that we were to know our sins forgiven on earth; supposing that it referred only to those to whom the Apostle was then writing, as I had never heard this doctrine preached in the Church. However, my prejudice quickly abated; and I plainly saw I could never be saved without knowing my sins were forgiven; and the Spirit of God sealed every word upon my heart. At the close of the discourse, however strange it may appear, a small still voice entered my heart with these words, "This is the truth!" and instantly I felt it in my soul.

My friend Greaves, observing my attention to the sermon, asked me how I liked Mr. Wesley. I replied, "As long as I live I will never part from him." I now broke off at a stroke from my old acquaintances in iniquity, who mocked and derided me exceedingly; and one of my most intimate acquaintances said to me, "What, Told! are you commenced a Whitefieldite? As sure as ever you were born, if you follow them you are damned." But the heavier my persecutions were, the more abundantly I rejoiced, and found such love and union to my Ministers, and companions in tribulation, that nought but death could make a separation.

I had now to encounter with my wife and family, with whom for many years I had lived peaceably; but they, perceiving an alteration in my behaviour, suspected that I had been among the Methodists. My wife, though a worthy, honest woman, yet an entire stranger to this light, one day exclaimed very warmly, and said, "What the d——l possesses you? I hope you have not been among the Methodists. I'll sacrifice my soul rather than you shall go among those miscreants." I gave her for answer, "If you are resolved to sacrifice your soul, I am resolved, God willing, to join them." At which she said no more, nor ever opposed my going to hear the word.

After this a very unfortunate circumstance happened. One evening, as my wife was occasionally at her accustomed chandler's shop, (which, in a course of years, had taken some hundreds of pounds of my wife's family,) she discovered a leg of pork roasting by the fire, and being big with her fourth child, longed to eat of it. Mr. C. was ever free with our family in what my house afforded; therefore my wife naturally imagined a similar degree of freedom on her part would not be considered as an act of rudeness by Mr. C. At this time, however, he seemed unfamiliar; nor did he invite my wife to partake of his supper as usual. Mrs. Told, being strictly modest, went home and informed her mother of the illiberality of Mr. C., who went immediately to him, and related to him my wife's condition; upon which he raved, swore, and replied, "What! can I not have a joint of meat but she must long for it?" Her mother, struck with his behaviour, quickly informed me thereof. I then went to him myself, and offered him half a guinea for a plate-ful of the pork, which he sharply refused. This broke off, for ever afterwards, our acquaintance; but I do not imagine that the disappointment would have affected my wife, had it not been principally owing to the weakness of her mother, who informed her of the man's cruel behaviour; which had so heavy an effect upon her, that the child became emaciated within her, insomuch that she was never delivered, but lay eight months under the Physician's care, which was attended with a very great expense. At this time my salary was but low, having no more than ten shillings per week.

In the year 1744, having been married seven years, my wife died, leaving only one child, a girl about two years of age. God now began to bless me in my outward circumstances. Soon after my wife's death, I was recommended to a Mr. Bembow, at Wapping, to serve him as a clerk, where I was greatly respected on account of my diligence in business. A few months of my services to Mr. Bembow were scarcely expired, before I was visited by Mr. Hogg, one of Mr. Wesley's stewards, who informed me, that Mr. Wesley requested my undertaking to teach the charity-children at the Foundery-School; but being fixed with Mr. Bembow, I refused it. A few days after, Mr. Hogg returned, and, together with a repetition of his former message, said that Mr. Wesley positively insisted upon it. I then believed it was my duty to comply with his desires, and therefore informed Mr. Bembow of the intended separation. Both Mr. Bembow and his wife entreated me to continue with them, telling me that no money should part us, as they never had an assistant who executed their commands with such attention; but believing it to be the will of God, I dared not to reject the undertaking, and therefore continued inexorable to their entreaties, though it was the occasion of much grief on both sides.

The day after I was established in the Foundery-School, and, in the space of a few weeks, collected threescore boys and six girls; but the society being poor, could not grant me more than ten shillings per week. This, however, was sufficient for me, as they boarded and clothed my daughter. Having the children under my care from five in the morning till five in the evening, both winter and summer, sparing no pains, with the assistance of an usher and four monitors, I brought near forty of them into writing and arithmetic. I continued in the school seven years and three months, and discharged two hundred and seventy-five boys, most of whom were fit for any trade.

In the year 1744, while I attended the children one morning at the five o'clock preaching, Mr. Wesley took his text out of the twenty-fifth chapter of St. Matthew, the forty-first and following verses. When he read these words, "I was sick, and in prison, and ye visited me not," as I was sensible of my negligence, in never visiting the prisoners during the course of my life, I was filled with horror of mind beyond expression. This drew me well nigh into a state of despondency, as I was totally unacquainted with the measures requisite to be pursued for that purpose. However, the gracious God, two or three days after, sent a messenger to me in the school, who informed me of ten malefactors that were under sentence of death, and would be glad of any of our friends who could make it convenient to go and pray with them. The messenger gave me to understand that they were all much awakened, and that one of them (John Lancaster) was converted, and full of the love of God. In consequence of this reviving information, I committed my school (without an hour's delay) to the superintendency of my usher, and went with the messenger to Newgate, where we had admittance into the cell wherein they were confined.

In the first place, I desired Lancaster to call them all together into his cell, and then began to inquire into the state of their souls. I addressed Lancaster first, as he appeared to be all alive to God. He told me that he had no doubt but that God, for Christ's sake, had forgiven him all his sins; and although (as he observed) he was very young, yet he had lived a very wicked life, and acknowledged, that three others, with himself, were the persons who robbed the Foundery one morning of all the brass candlesticks; but he knew that, shortly, he should be with Jesus in paradise. He added, "This morning, about five o'clock, the Sun of Righteousness arose in my dark cell; and I am now so full of God and Heaven, and I am like a barrel of new wine, ready to bust for vent. O for words to express what I now feel!" I then spoke to the rest, six of whom seemed clear of their acceptance in the Beloved.

While I was speaking to these, one Roberts, a carman, who lived in White-cross-street, entered the cell, looking at me with a sullen shyness, and with a countenance speaking the very spirit of the old serpent dwelling in him. This immediately struck me, and I endeavoured to speak to him with comfortable words, and to use the most pacific exhortations I was capable of, inviting him to come to the Lord Jesus as a poor, helpless, lost, and undone sinner. I told him that Jesus was the sinner's only Friend; that the King of Heaven laid down His life for the chief of sinners; and that He certainly died for him: I therefore quoted (for example) David, Mary Magdalene, Peter, and the thief on the cross. While I was thus speaking to him, I perceived his countenance to change into a smile, and his savage behaviour transformed into a child-like deportment. God instantly made the lion to lie down with the kid; for this turbulent man became meek, and continued so till his last moments.

The report having been made, and the death-warrant coming down, eight of the ten were ordered for execution; the other two were respited: neither of these appeared to have the least concern for his soul; but I trust they were spared for a good purpose, that they might have a little more time for repentance.

The day being arrived when the other eight malefactors were to die, another person and myself were early at the cell, in order to render them all the service in our power. The keeper having received directions over night to lock them all up in one cell, that they might pour out their souls together in fervent prayer to Almighty God, it proved a happy night to each of them; so that when they were led down from their cell, they appeared like giants refreshed with wine: there was no fear of death apparent in their countenances. Upon being called out to have their irons taken off, Lancaster was the first. While they were doing it, the Sheriff being present, Lancaster looked up to Heaven with a pleasant smile, and said, "Glory be to God for the first moment of my entrance into this place; for before I came hither, my heart was as hard as the wall, and my soul as black as hell; but, O! I am now washed from all my sins, and by one o'clock shall be with Jesus in paradise;" and, with many strong expressions, he exhorted the innumerable spectators to flee from the wrath to come. This caused the Sheriff to shed tears, being greatly affected with Lancaster's lively and animated spirit. They were a long time getting off the last man's fetters. When they were gotten off, Lancaster, beholding him at a short distance, clapped his hands together, and said, "Here comes another of our little flock." A gentleman present said, "I think it is too great a flock upon such an occasion." Lancaster said, "O no, it is not too great a flock for such a Shepherd as Jesus; there is room enough in Heaven for us all." Then he exhorted the populace to forsake their sins, pressed them to come to the throne of grace immediately; assuring them, that they would find God gracious and merciful to forgive them, as He had forgiven him.

At length they were ordered into the cart, and I was prevailed upon to go with them. When we were in the cart, I addressed myself to each of them separately. The first person was Atkins, a youth of nineteen years of age. I said to him, "Are you afraid to die?" He replied, "No, sir; I really am not." I then asked him, "Wherefore he was not afraid to die?" He answered, "Because I have laid my soul at the feet of Jesus." I then spoke to Gardner, a journeyman carpenter, about the age of fifty, who made a very comfortable report of what the Lord had done for his soul, in the remission of all his past sins; for he found the peace of God in his heart. The last person to whom I spoke was one Thompson, a very illiterate young man; but he also had no fear of death: assuring me that he was perfectly happy in his Saviour, and continued so till his last moments.

This was the first time of my visiting the malefactors at Newgate, and of my attending them to the place of execution; and it was not without much shame, because I perceived the greater part of the populace considered me as one of the sufferers. When we came to the fatal tree, Lancaster lifted up his eyes thereto, and said, "Blessed be God!" then prayed extempore in a very excellent manner, and the others behaved with great discretion. John Lancaster had no friend to procure him a proper interment; so that when they had hung the usual time, and were cut down, the surgeon's mob secured his body, and carried it over to Paddington. When the mob was dispersed, a remarkable occurrence took place:—

A company of eight sailors, with truncheons in their hands, looked up to the gallows with an angry countenance, the bodies having been cut down some minutes previous to their arrival. An old woman, who sold gin, observing them to grow violent, by reason of their disappointment, mildly said, "Gentlemen, I suppose you want the man that the surgeons have got." "Ay," replied the sailors, "where is he?" She told them that the surgeon's crew had carried them over to Paddington, and pointed out to them the road thither. They hastened away, and as they entered the town, inquired where the surgeon's mob was. On receiving the information they wanted, they went and demanded the body of John Lancaster. When they had obtained it, two of them took him on their shoulders, and carried it round by Islington. They being tired, two others laid themselves under the body, and carried it from thence to Shoreditch; then two more carried it from Shoreditch to Coverlet's-fields; at length, after they were all weary, and unable to carry it farther, they agreed to lay it on the step of the first door they came to. They did so, and went their way. This gave birth to a great riot in the neighbour-hood, which brought an old woman, who had lived in the house, down stairs. When she saw the corpse at the step of the door, she cried out, "Lord, here is my son, John Lancaster!" This being spread abroad, the Methodists made a collection, and got him a shroud and a coffin. This event was the more singular, as the seamen had no knowledge of the body, nor to whom he belonged when living. My second wife went with me to see him previous to the burial; but neither of us could perceive the least alteration in his visage or features, or any appearance of violence on any part of his body. A pleasant smile appeared in his countenance, and he lay as in a sweet sleep.

From the time of my introduction among the prisoners, I preached frequently to the felons and debtors in Newgate. Of the latter I joined about thirty-six in a regular society; nor would they suffer an individual to live in any outward sin, as they never neglected to inform me of every such instance. I had so lively a zeal for the cause of religion, from my first hearing the Gospel, that I spared no pains to do all the good in my power, both to the bodies and souls of sinners; embracing every opportunity, both in hearing and speaking; so that in process of time I preached in every prison, as well as many workhouses, in and about London; and frequently travelled to almost every town within twelve miles of the Metropolis.

I still continued in the Foundery-School; and by my second marriage, my family was much increased in temporal circumstances, and my soul was exceedingly delighted; but by rising at four o'clock every morning, going to the five o'clock preaching, diligently attending the Church service, and strictly observing all the other ordinances of God, I was more deeply convinced of my unbelief, and the remains of the carnal mind. No tongue can express the bitterness of soul I now laboured under, both day and night having "no rest in my flesh, by reason of my sin;" and although my place of abode joined the Foundery, yet when I have left the school to go either to breakfast or dinner, my agony of mind has been so great, that I have even forgot to eat my bread, and oftentimes wandered into Hoxton-fields, to pour out my misery before God. Frequently, after I had dismissed my scholars in the evening, I have taken a solitary walk into the fields till nine, ten, and eleven o'clock, roaring for the very disquietude of my soul; and notwithstanding I never could accuse myself of inattention to any ordinance, fasting and praying, &c., yet my unbelief prevailed, till I became completely miserable.

In this situation I continued about three years, so that I chose "strangling rather than life;" nor could I, with all my hearing and self-denial, overcome this damning sin of unbelief. When people told me I could believe if I would, gladly would I have given worlds to believe, were they in my power; but "such power belongeth to God alone;" and glory be to Him, He at last displayed that power in my deliverance; the manner of which I shall now simply and sincerely relate. Taking one morning my melancholy walk, after five o'clock preaching, as I was passing Ratcliff-row I perceived a cow coming towards me, and really wished in my heart that I was that beast, as I considered it ten thousand times happier than myself. The next thing that passed me was a dog; when I wished I could change myself into that animal. Afterwards I observed a man a few yards off, and thought he would afford me the greatest happiness, if he would put an end to my wretched life.

In these miserable moments I had no conception of a deliverance near; especially as the enemy of my soul suggested to me, that if I lived five hundred years in the world, I should never receive a change of spirit by the grace of God. I continued walking till I came to a lonesome part of a field, by the Shepherd and Shepherdess, which I imagined was better calculated for retirement than any other spot thereabouts. When I had secluded myself therein, on a sudden, in the twinkling of an eye, a hand struck me on the top of my head, which affected me very much; but I instantly found myself crying with a loud voice, "Praise God, praise God!" and looking up, I beheld the sky, as it were, full of the glory of God. This attended me for the space of a minute, but was succeeded by an uncommon thick darkness. I did not feel any pain, but it was followed with these words, "This is one of your old delusions." I was staggered at this for a few moments; yet was quickly enabled to look up to heaven, and to beseech God, in fervent prayer, that I might more fully know whether this was a sign of the remission of sins. As I looked up, the heavens seemed to open about a mile in length, and tapered away to a point at each end. The centre of this avenue was about twelve feet wide, wherein I thought I saw the Lord Jesus standing, holding both His hands up, from the palms of which the blood seemed to stream down. Floods of tears now gushed from my eyes, and trickled down my cheeks; and I said, "Lord, it is enough!"

Chapter Eight

NOTHING remarkable having occurred in my spiritual or temporal affairs, from the year 1745 to 1775, I shall now give a further account of my labours among the prisoners in Newgate.

I believe it is upwards of twenty-one years since I first attended the prisoners in Newgate, both debtors and felons; and was there a witness of the horrible scene, which is the very emblem of the infernal pit. Having a constant pressure upon my mind to stand up for God in the midst of them, I prayed for wisdom and fortitude, as it is so disagreeable a task to flesh and blood. For a few years, I met with many repulses from the keepers and Ordinary, and also from the prisoners themselves; but I the more vehemently pressed through all; so that (in the name of God) I would take no denial.

The Ordinary constantly, on Sunday morning, stationed himself a few doors from Newgate, for the space of two hours and more, to obstruct my entrance; forbidding all the turn-keys to give me admittance: yet the God of all compassion frequently made an entrance for me, so that I had an opportunity of preaching every Sunday morning on the debtor's side, to the number of forty prisoners, who behaved with much seriousness and attention; after which I proposed the uniting themselves together in a society. I read and left with them the Rules of our Society, desiring them to consider seriously, whether they deemed it proper to confine themselves to such regulations or not. On my next visit I understood that, through the circumspection of two or three prisoners, who were men of understanding, and of a liberal education, and who highly approved of my proposals, an unity had taken place among thirty or more of them. For a considerable time they paid regular attention to preaching, and to the meeting of the society. If any offence was given, I was made acquainted with it. This economy continued for a considerable time, when a tumult was made by the Ordinary, who ever afterwards shut me out from these parts of the prison; yet there was a blessed work of God's Spirit among the felons; and more eminently among the condemned malefactors.

One instance was one Holmes, who was very useful to his fellow-sufferers, and likewise to the spectators. Having no opposition, I joyfully embraced the opportunity of visiting him and five other malefactors, and soon gained their attention to my arguments to seek salvation by faith in Christ.

Here I endeavoured to take such methods of conducting myself towards these men as I had usually done with the former happy departed souls; and as I had an open door into the cells, which ever proved the most beneficial to the then confined prisoners, I went from cell to cell, and was locked in with each of them for a longer or shorter time, according to the state of their mind. Herein the hand of the Almighty was evident. Finding Holmes more lively and active than any of the rest, he answered a very useful purpose; having a clear sense of forgiveness himself, he zealously exerted himself in bringing the rest of his fellow-sufferers to a true sense of the necessity of being born again: and truly the Lord prospered his endeavours, so that every visit I made, I found the rest of the malefactors either under strong convictions, or just ready to step into the pool. The advice I gave them was principally intended to make them more deeply sensible of their lost estate, and I was very cautious of daubing them with untempered mortar; and hence I always perceived their conversions were more solid, real, and permanent: so that what they had received was truly shown in their conduct. A few days before their death, I came more home to the point, and showed how impossible it was to be happy, either in time or eternity, without God being reconciled to them through the death of our Lord Jesus Christ, and a sense of the forgiveness of their sins. None of them appeared to be clear on this point except Holmes.

Here I was struck with the conduct of one of the young men, a Roman Catholic, who, notwithstanding all I could say, would not be reconciled to his prosecutor, declaring that he would maintain that resolution to his last moments! I told him, the word of God lay flat against him, quoting that passage of Scripture, "If ye from your heart forgive not every one his brother his trespasses, neither will your heavenly Father forgive your trespasses." This greatly alarmed him, so that he became more teachable. The night before their execution, I desired the inner keeper to give them the opportunity of assembling together in one cell, to the end they might all pass their last hours in pouring out their souls in fervent prayer before God: this was granted. I also requested one of the prisoners, who had been confined for some years, to attend them diligently, and read to them. He did so; and accordingly they began their exercise out of the Prayer-book; but after a while, one of them said, "Come, let us pray extempore; and who knows but God will open our mouths?" They all gladly consented; and the Lord in mercy did not only open their mouths, but their hearts too, and that in an unusual manner, manifesting himself unto them as he does not unto the world; so that they wrestled with God in such fervour of spirit, from nine till twelve o'clock, that each of them was in a profuse sweat. Then they laid themselves down to rest from twelve to two, when every one of them joined in prayer; nor did they desist from that exercise till the time arrived when they were summoned to chapel.

I went that morning before day-light, and availed myself of the opportunity of getting admittance just before they were let down. As they entered the press-yard, I saw the happy consequence of their last acts of devotion. No tongue or pen is able to represent the solemn joy and peace which appeared in each countenance, particularly in the young Roman Catholic, whom I could not prevail upon to forgive his prosecutor. To him I chiefly addressed myself, saying, "My dear man, how do you find yourself?" He replied, with a pleasant voice, and a heavenly countenance, "Find myself! why truly, Sir, my soul is filled with light, love, and peace, that I am the same as if I had nothing beside within me!" In this rapturous spirit he continued to his last moments. After chapel, Holmes, with the others, came down, and had their irons struck off. He spoke to all about him of the unspeakable love of God to him; and assured them that he knew God, for Christ's sake, had forgiven all his sins. His words were so powerful, that he drew abundance of tears from the spectators. After they were haltered, they were put into the three carts, and sent for execution. I went with Holmes in the first, spending our time to the most advantage. Upon our arrival at the tree, Holmes first stood up, and, lifting his eyes to heaven, said, "Lord, didst Thou not die for sinners? Thou didst die for me!" Then, turning round to the multitude, he prayed extempore, so that it caused hundreds to be in tears around the gallows. When prayers were finished by the Ordinary, all of them, agreeable to my request, went off the stage of mortality, first turning round, and putting their faces to each other, their hands being tied, crying out, as in the voice of one man, "Lord Jesus, receive our spirits."

During the space of time between the several executions, I frequently preached and exhorted among the felons and debtors in Newgate, and constantly visited the sick in all parts of the prison; which I have reason to believe was blessed, in a great measure, to many of their souls; as numbers were prepared to receive the glad tidings of salvation when under sentence of death.

Some years ago, Morgan, Whalley, Brett, and Dupree, with two more, being under sentence of death, were ordered for execution; and though they were all conspicuous characters in life, yet the highest interest the nation could afford was ineffectual to obtain as exemption from justice.

The circumstance was thus:—They all agreed upon a party of pleasure, at the election of a Member for Chelmsford, in Essex; and after they had glutted themselves with immoderate eating and drinking, they consented to divert themselves by going out upon the road, and robbing the first person they should meet. A farmer chanced to pass, whom they attacked and robbed of all his money. The farmer having met with assistance, pursued them into Chelmsford, where they were secured, and removed to London. Here they were cast, received sentence of death, and ordered for execution. Mr. Brett was the son of an eminent Divine in Dublin; Whalley, a gentleman of considerable fortune; Dupree was also a gentleman; and Morgan, an officer on board one of His Majesty's ships of war. The last of these was frequently visited by Lady B. H., (the Duke of Hamilton's daughter,) both before and after sentence. As I was often present with them at their several interviews in Newgate, I understood, if this affair had not happened, Mr. Morgan and Lady Betty were to have been married in a very short time.

This lady went daily to His Majesty, as did also others who had great influence, and pleaded with His Majesty for the life of Mr. Morgan; but His Majesty, considering it a point of injustice, as well as partiality, would by no means attend to her petitions. Besides, as they were all persons of fortune, and could not plead necessity. His Majesty said, his subjects were not to be put in fear, and to suffer the loss of their property, merely through a wanton whim. However, the morning before the execution, Lady B. H. appeared before His Majesty, and fell upon her knees. "My Lady," said His Majesty, "there is no end to your importunity: I will spare his life, upon condition that he be not acquainted therewith till he arrives at the place of execution." Accordingly, Brett, Whalley, and Dupree were tied up to the gallows; the other cart, with Morgan, and two other gentlemen, followed; but the Sheriff, upon ordering the coach to stop, produced the respite sent to Morgan from His Majesty. It is hard to express the alarm this made among the multitude; and when I turned round and saw one of the prisoners out of the cart, falling to the ground, he having fainted away at the sudden news, I was instantly seized with terror, as I thought it was a rescue rather than a reprieve; but when I beheld Morgan put into a coach, and perceived that Lady Betty Hamilton was seated therein, in order to receive him, my fear was at an end.

As soon as the coach, with Morgan and the lady, had drove off, a venerable gentleman walked up to the first cart, and addressing himself to Dupree, begged him to look steadfastly to God, in whose presence he would shortly appear; and hoped the mercy his companion received would have no bad effect upon him. Dupree, with calmness and composure of mind, said "Sir, I thank God that he is thus reprieved; it does not by any means affect me." This gave the gentleman much satisfaction. When prayers were ended, I addressed each of them in the most awful words I was capable of, and have reason to believe they were not in vain, as they all appeared entirely resigned to their fate. Brett, in a mild spirit, earnestly craved the prayers of the multitude, and conjured them to take warning by the untimely end of the three objects of their present attention. When they were turned off, and the mob nearly dispersed, I hastened back to Newgate, and there seriously conversed with Mr. Morgan, who, in consequence of the unexpected change, was scarcely recovered.

In the course of our conversation he told me, that a few minutes before, and at the arrival of the reprieve, he was in so happy a state, that he could not tell whether life or death was most desirable. Yet, when about six weeks were elapsed, it evidently appeared that the impression made by His Majesty's gracious act of lenity was clearly worn off; for one day I detected him in playing at cards with one Mr. Barrett, who was confined on suspicion of defrauding his creditors, and who seemed to be totally destitute of the fear or knowledge of God, and was also very prejudicial in his behaviour to the souls of poor condemned prisoners, ever attempting to divert their minds from their attention to that which was truly good; likewise setting at nought and exposing to ridicule those who incessantly laboured for their eternal benefit. I then laid before Mr. Morgan the dangerous folly of such proceedings, and added, "If such conduct as that" (namely, playing at cards) "is abolished by men of common sense, how much more then ought it to be so by one who had so recently been rescued from death by His Majesty's clemency!" I therefore entreated him to lay the cards aside, and never attempt to resume them any more. By this remonstrance he became very complaisant; and, in a moment's time he paid attention to all my reproofs.

Mr. Barrett began to abuse me very much, because I had interrupted their playing. Shortly after, his creditors, having suspicion that he had some effects concealed in Newgate, obtained an order to search it, and found to the amount of five thousand pounds in bank-notes, cut in halves. Soon after this his trial came on, and he was found guilty. He, with Mr. Samuel Lee, who was condemned for forgery, were ordered for execution; Barrett, on Tuesday, in Smithfield; Lee, on Wednesday, at Tyburn. Barrett refused my company, and the service I might have been to him; therefore I cannot give any account of his behaviour during his last moments; but Lee was very attentive to instruction, and just before he was turned off put a letter into my hand, which I opened, and was deeply affected with the contents. It began thus, "Oh, eternity! eternity! eternity! who can fathom the depths of eternity?" The whole of the letter expressed the devoutest sentiments of his soul. His behaviour on the passage to and at the place of execution was altogether serious; nor did he leave room to doubt of his eternal salvation.

I shall next speak of what I heard and knew of Mary Edmonson, who was executed on Kennington Common, on suspicion of murdering her aunt at Rotherhithe. This unfortunate young woman was under close confinement a long time. When the day arrived, she was conveyed to Kingston, to be tried before Judge Dennison, who, some time before, tried a Mr. Coleman, a brewer's clerk, for the supposed abuse of a young woman; and although the opponents of Mr. Coleman laboured to persuade this young woman that Coleman was the person who treated her in that scandalous manner, yet when they were in each other's presence, she declared he was not the man. His enemies still pressed upon this young woman to change her opinion, assuring her that he was the offender; and as further interrogatories were put to her, respecting the circumstances which had been alleged, she gave a contradictory answer, which seemed to imply that he was the man: he was therefore put into confinement, and there secured till his trial came on, when he was condemned, and executed. About three years after this, Mr. Coleman's innocence was brought to light; the carman who drove him to the place of execution having been proved to be the man, and that by his own confession: he was therefore tried, condemned, and executed; and one Mr. Delagourd, who was found perjured in Coleman's case, was sentenced to stand in the pillory, opposite St. George's church, in the Borough. Afterwards he, with two others who were concerned in the taking away Mr. Coleman's life, were transported.

I return now to Mary Edmonson. She was tried by Judge

Dennison upon mere circumstances, as no positive evidence against her could be produced. However, the prisoner suffered very severe and rigorous treatment from the Judge, because she insisted upon her innocence and integrity, the Judge still laying the murder to her charge, calling her a notorious, vile wretch, assuring her that she would be d—d if she denied the fact, as matters were so evident, particularly as her apron and cap were found covered with blood in the copper-hole: but she was condemned on circumstances only. As I attended her to the place of execution, I have reason to believe she was innocent of the charge.

As I was prevented from visiting this woman while in confinement, I did not expect to see her suffer; but as I was passing through the Borough, I called on a Mr. Skinner, a cheesemonger, in that street, who earnestly entreated me to attend her, that being the morning appointed for her execution. I complied with his entreaties, although I was extremely fatigued by a long journey; and as he further observed, that the unhappy woman had been brutally dealt with in the course of her imprisonment, and also greatly hindered in making her peace with God, I immediately set out for Kennington Common, yet with little hopes of getting to speak to her before she entered into her unchangeable state. Some minutes previous to my arrival near the Common where she was to suffer, Thomas Tollis, the executioner, espied me, and, filled with joy and tears, hurried through the crowd, and said, "Mr. Told, I thank God you are come: pray follow me, and I will lead you to the room wherein she will shortly be confined; and, for God's sake, speak as closely to her as you can."

I followed him into the room, and having tarried about the space of half-an-hour, I heard a violent shout of "Here she comes!" I then went to the window which looked into the road, and there perceived that the mob were giving her a shocking reception, by terrible curses and oaths. When the prisoner was brought into the room, she stood with her back against the wainscot, and appeared perfectly resigned to the will of God. I then addressed her, saying, "My dear, for God's sake, for Christ's sake, and for the sake of your own precious soul, do not die with a lie in your mouth! You are, in a few moments, to appear in the presence of a holy God, who is of purer eyes than to behold iniquity. O consider what an eternity of misery must be; and this will be the certain portion of all who die in their sins: therefore, if you are guilty, openly confess it; or, if you were in any wise concerned in the murder, you are not clear before God, if you do not publicly acknowledge your guilt." She heard me with much meekness and simplicity; but answered, that she had already advanced the truth, and hoped she should persevere in the same spirit to her last moment. Mr. Hammett, who was then chief keeper of the New Prison, by order of the Sheriff, dismissed every person out of the room; and said to me, "Mr. Told, I am sensible of the business upon which you came hither; but must beg you will quit the room, as no person is permitted to attend her without obtaining the Sheriff's consent;" but, upon Mr. Hammett's following me out, he intimated that the Sheriff would grant me permission to attend her in the cart to the place of execution, if I deemed it prudent to ask him.

The time of her departure for the gallows having arrived, I solicited the Sheriff's permission to visit her as soon as possible. He asked me if I was a Clergyman. I replied, "No, Sir." "Are you a Dissenting Minister?" I answered, "No." "What are you then?" I informed him, that I was one who preached the Gospel, and could wish to be the means of bringing the prisoner to a confession. He then desired me to lay hold of his horse's bridle, and told me I should accompany her to the place of execution; yet he did not urge me to rush into that dangerous attempt immediately, seeing the rioters were so exasperated against her. As we were proceeding on the road, the Sheriff's horse being close to the cart, I looked at her from under the horse's bridle, and said, "My dear, look to Jesus." This advice quickened her spirit, insomuch, that although she did not look about her before, yet she then turned herself round to me, and joyfully answered, "Sir, I bless God, I can look to Jesus, to my comfort." This produced a pleasant smile in her countenance, which when the sons of violence perceived, they d——d her in a shameful manner; this was accompanied with a vengeful shout, "See how bold she is! See how the b——h laughs!"

At length we came to the gallows, where many officers were stationed on horseback, besides numbers more on foot, furnished with constables' staves. When the cart was backed under the gallows, a very corpulent man trod on my left foot with such weight, that I really thought he had taken it quite off: however, the Sheriff soon cleared the way, and formed an arrangement of constables round the cart; then directed some of them to put me into it, in order that I might be of all the service to the malefactor in my power; the Sheriff himself standing behind the cart, the better to avail himself of my discourse with her. When she was tied up, I began to press her to acknowledge the murder, in the most solemn manner I was capable; but she declared her innocence in presence of the Sheriff. I then interrogated her. "Did you not commit the fact? Had you no concern therein? Were you not interested in the murder?" She answered, "I am as clear of the whole affair as I was the day my mother brought me into the world." The Sheriff, on hearing these words, shed plenty of tears, and said, "Good God! it is a second Coleman's case!" This circumstance likewise brought tears from many persons who heard her.

When I was getting out of the cart, the executioner put the handkerchief over her eyes; but she quickly moved it away, and addressing herself to the multitude, begged them to pray that God would bring to light, when she was departed, the cause of the assassination; saying, that she had no doubt but that the prayers of such persons would be heard; and repeated her innocence, solemnly declaring that she was as ignorant of the crime for which she was going to suffer, as at the day of her birth; and added also, "I do not lay anything to the charge of my Maker; He has an undoubted right to take me out of this world as seemeth Him good; and although I am clear of this murder, yet I have sinned against Him in many grievous instances; but I bless God, He hath forgiven me all my sins." Her kinsman then came up into the cart, and would fain have saluted her; but she mildly turned her face aside, strongly suspecting him to be the assassin, having frequently challenged him therewith at Kingston.

After her kinsman was gone out of the cart, the executioner, a second time, was putting the handkerchief over her face, which she again turned aside, looking at the Sheriff, lamenting thus with meekness, "I think it cruel that none is suffered to pray by me." The Sheriff then desired me, for God's sake, to go a second time into the cart, and renew my prayers with her; which, when finished, she began to pray extempore, and in a most excellent manner. When she had concluded her prayer, the executioner performed his part, and being turned off, her body dropped against my right shoulder, nor did she once struggle or move, but she was as still as if she had hung three hours.

Upon her trial it was represented that she cut all her fingers across on both hands for deception, in order to lay the murder upon some other person: but in her defence upon trial, she declared that her fingers were not cut by a knife; but being alarmed, when she entered the house at seeing four men, one of whom was in a white frock; and also seeing her aunt lie weltering in her own blood, she started, which when the murderers perceived, they all ran out of doors. Mary followed them closely, caught the door with both her hands, and called out, "Murder;" but, by her pulling the door very hard, her eight fingers were thereby jammed almost off. When she was executed, I noticed her fingers, went immediately and took a door, with which I jammed my fingers also, and found them to be marked exactly like hers.

I now return to the kinsman of Mary Edmonson, who upon the death of his aunt (as Mary and he were cousins) was entitled to a hundred pounds, left him by way of legacy, and likewise Mary to two hundred pounds. The kinsman having received his, bought himself out of the army. Some time after the execution of his kinswoman, he, with another man, hired a post-chaise in the Borough, to go on a party of pleasure to Croydon Fair. Upon their return in the evening, Mary Edmonson's kinsman said to his friend in the chaise, as passing Kennington gallows, "There is the place where my kinswoman was hung wrongfully!" The other (struck by the assertion) said, "Wrongfully! how do you know she was hung wrongfully?" "Because," replied the kinsman, "I should have gone in her room." His companion, after a short conversation, asked him where was the place of his abode? He answered, "In Hedge-lane, Charing-Cross." When they had put up the chaise, the supposed friend of Mary's kinsman went that moment to Justice Hammond, in the Borough; who, being informed of what had passed, granted a warrant to apprehend him. He was accordingly apprehended, and committed to Newgate, where, at his request, I visited him. He then desired me to render him all the spiritual assistance I was able; but my instructions were lost by the advice which he received at Newgate from his fellow-criminals, having speedily learned to deny the confession he had made to his companion in the chaise. Notwithstanding this, he was removed from Newgate to Kingston, and tried before Judge Dennison, who tried his kinswoman, Mary Edmonson; but as he denied the charge, the Judge acquitted him: however, he soon went on the highway, and committed a robbery, for which he was tried, cast, and condemned; but I have been informed, Judge Dennison, to prevent clamours, got him a reprieve for transportation.

I shall next give an account of Harris, who was reported to be "the flying highwayman." During his confinement after sentence, he was both stupid and hardened, inattentive to

instruction from the Ordinary or myself. The morning of
his execution, when he came out of the cell, he behaved as
a man deprived of his senses; and upon entering the chapel,
he became so violent, that the Ordinary was affrighted, and
ran away: however, I went to him, and endeavoured to set
before him the awful eternity he was just going to enter
into; yet all the counsel I gave him was as water spilled upon
the ground; nor was the least sign of repentance to be seen
in his countenance or behaviour. The others that were
sentenced to suffer with him, were ordered into the cart, yet
still the same stupidity of mind remained in Harris; nor did
he give the least attention to what was spoken to him, until
we had passed a little beyond Hatton-garden: I then pressed
him to be silent for the space of ten minutes, during which
to be very observant in keeping the eye of his mind steadfastly fixed on the ever-blessed and adorable Jesus, and to
beseech Him to forgive all his sins. Hanging back his head
on the cart, he shut his eyes, and was profoundly silent for
the space of ten minutes; when, raising himself up, and the
tears pouring down his cheeks, he clapped his hands together,
and said "Now I know the Lord Jesus has forgiven me all
my sins, and I have nothing to do but to die." He then
burst into an extempore prayer, that the populace might
distinctly hear him on all sides, and continued happy to his
last moment. He solemnly denied his being the flying highwayman, as he never leaped a turnpike-gate in his life; yet
acknowledged that he had committed several highway
robberies.

Chapter Nine

THE next person of whom I shall give an account is one Anderson, a poor labouring man, whose character until now was unimpeachable, touching his industry, sobriety, and honesty. He had a wife far gone with child, and a daughter about seven years old: but was totally destitute of money, clothes, and a spot where to lay their heads; having been, by one of their rigid creditors, dispossessed of the mean habitation they formerly held, and necessitated to lie on the floor in such places as they were permitted.

One morning, having been long without employment, he said to his wife, "My dear, I have a strong inclination to go down upon the quays: it may be the Lord will provide for me a loaf of bread, or some employment, whereby we may sustain ourselves a little longer, or else we shall perish with hunger." He accordingly went out; but, finding all resources fail, temptation entered into his mind to commence robber. Accordingly he went into Hoxton-fields, where meeting two washerwomen, who were bringing home their clean linen, he, without bidding them stop, said to one, "Mistress, I want money." She replied, "I have only two-pence." "Then," said he, "give me that." After this he addressed the other,

"You have got money, I know you have." The woman answered, "I have but fourpence." He took that likewise, and, scarce knowing what he did, he walked before them into town. When they arrived in Old-street, the two women called a constable, and both declared that he stopped them in Hoxton-fields, and robbed them of their money. He was committed to prison, tried, and cast at the Old Bailey, with several others, who lay a considerable time under sentence before the report was made to His Majesty.

In the interim poor Mrs. Anderson, though big with her third child, made frequent visits to her husband; and, through the pity of some friends, was enabled to supply him with food. During the many years I attended the prisoners, I have not seen such meek, loving, and tender spirits as appeared in the countenance and deportment of this poor man and his wife. Indeed, they were naturally inclined to few words; but the woman frequently seating herself by her husband's side, and throwing her arms round his neck, they would shed floods of tears to mitigate the anguish which overwhelmed their united hearts: but it is impossible to do justice to their exquisite sensibility and tender affection. When I called the prisoners into the press-yard room, they behaved with the deepest attention; nor do I remember to have made them one visit but I found their souls to be greatly profited by my exhortations.

Some time before the death-warrant came down, Anderson was both convinced of sin, and also made sensible of the remission of it. The morning of his execution being arrived, I attended him a little past six o'clock, and upon his being let down from his cell, found him to be exceedingly happy in his mind. He said he had no doubt of his salvation, and that he should shortly be with Jesus, whom his soul loved; and added, "This is the happiest day I ever saw in my life. O! who can express the joy and peace I now feel! If I could have all the world, I would not wish to live another day!" The Minister, churchwardens, and overseers, with several others of St.

Luke's parish, presented various petitions to His Majesty on his behalf, and he had an honourable character from the Captain of the man-of-war whereto he formerly belonged, and from which he was regularly discharged; yet when his case was under the consideration of the Privy Council, by a wrong information which they received, that he was the Anderson who was an audacious highwayman at that time, he was included in the death-warrant.

As I was going in the cart with him to the place of execution, knowing the miserable situation of his wife, I inquired of him where she was to be found; to which he answered, "I can give you no kind of intelligence, as she has no place of abode, but lies on the floor in some poor person's house, moving from house to house, as she is compelled by necessity." I then asked him where there might be a probability of discovering her. He told me in Lamb-alley, Bishopsgate-street. I spent therefore three days in grovelling through almost every dirty alley in that neighbourhood; and after having almost given up hope of finding her, I at last received information that she dwelt in Holywell-lane. I went there accordingly, and found her in a melancholy situation, sitting with a poor old woman; when looking into the room, I saw no other furniture than a piece of old rug, whereon they both laid themselves to sleep; the room also was, I verily believe, more nauseous than the cell of Newgate. When I had spoken a few words, I gave her directions to call at my house in Christopher's-alley. She came, but not without much fear, imagining I had something against her.

As I was engaged in other employment when she came to my house, my wife put two shillings into her hand, bidding her also come and take a dinner. In the course of their conversation, my wife observed to Mrs. Anderson that I only wanted to do her all the good that was in my power. The next night I was appointed to preach in Old-Gravel-lane, where I represented to the congregation the unfortunate case of Mr. Anderson, who died for sixpence, being his first crime.

I also set forth the afflicted and deplorable situation of his wife. And although the congregation that evening was but small, and those chiefly poor people, yet they contributed to her relief six-and-twenty shillings; and, by laying her case before others, I got her as much as clothed her decently. As I perceived that she began to grow near her time, I asked her if she could give me an account of the parish she properly belonged to, telling her I would get her a petition signed by one of the Governors of the London Lying-in-Hospital, to provide for her reception; but the poor woman not having any knowledge of her husband's parish, I was therefore obliged to commit her as one of the casual poor on the parish of Shoreditch. Doctor Watham informed me she could not be admitted into the London Lying-in-Hospital without a security from the parish, to receive the child in case of her death.

I then waited on the principal churchwarden; but he being absent, I went to the other, who ridiculed and abused me in the most scandalous manner, although I had already represented to him the lamentable state of Mrs. Anderson, assuring him that her life would be lost for want of attention, being left entirely destitute of money or clothing. The savage replied, "I suppose it is some woman you have got with child, and you want to father it upon the parish." I told him I lived but a few doors from him; that my character was well known; and if he chose to inquire thereinto, he would, in my opinion, find himself mistaken. He then said, in a surly manner, "Then I suppose it is some hanged man's widow or other." I took my leave of him, and hastened immediately to a gentleman, an acquaintance of the upper churchwarden, and informed him of the unkind behaviour of the other with the distressed situation of poor Mrs. Anderson. The upper churchwarden desired my friend to send her to his house the next morning by eight o'clock. She waited on him accordingly, and he ordered her in, and gave her a good breakfast, while he signed her petition. When he had so done, he ordered her to carry it to the under churchwarden to sign it also, at whose peril it would be to refuse her, seeing the upper churchwarden had previously signed it. As soon as her petition was signed, she attended at the hospital in Aldersgate-street, and was admitted, where, in a few days, she was delivered of a fine girl. When her month was elapsed, my wife received her into our own house, with the child, and she continued there for many months, performing her daily business industriously, with all sobriety and cleanliness. Some time after, her child died, and I procured a house-keeper's place for her, where she gave great satisfaction, and soon became a creditable woman. I also bound her daughter an apprentice to a weaver.

Some time after Mr. Anderson's execution, I attended Mr. Powell, who was cast for forgery. He was much of the gentleman, as well as a very personable man. The only observation I have to make on his behaviour is, that during his confinement, seriousness and devotion were truly conspicuous in him. He never failed to instruct his brethren under his unhappy situation; so that, by his upright walking in the fear of God, a solemn awe was laid on the minds of those of his fellow-sufferers. When the day appointed for execution arrived, the Sheriff indulged him with a coach, and bade me get therein, that I might dispense my spiritual labour to this invaluable soul. I accordingly exerted myself to the utmost in giving him this kind of help; and afterwards went to the other malefactors, who were conveyed in carts, and there attended them also, imparting similar passages of scriptural assistance to them. Mr. Powell's mind was stayed upon God in so steadfast a manner, that after we had sung a hymn, and concluded our prayers, he closed his eyes, and earnestly entreated me to decline my discourse with him, in order that he might be the better enabled to meditate on God, and an awful eternity. At the place of execution they all behaved with that penitence and solemnity naturally expected of men going into an unchangeable state;

therefore, I humbly hope they are all lodged in Immanuel's breast.

In the next place I shall speak of Mr. Gibson, an attorney, who was sentenced to death for forgery. He was an eminent character in his profession, and handsome in his person. In respect to his religious principles, he had been very wavering and irresolute, ever learning, but never coming to the perfect knowledge of the truth: sometimes he inclined to the Romish Church, at other times he would conform to the established Church of England: then he would go with the Methodists; and sometimes he held with the Dissenters of various denominations: but I soon became acquainted with his motives for this kind of doctrine-hunting, viz., that it arose from pecuniary views and lucrative designs; this I learned by his own acknowledgment. He frequently attended my exhortations with the rest under sentence, always expressing much satisfaction thereby. I also made him repeated visits to his own room, where he always received me with expressions of pleasure.

Upon his trial, his cause had been referred to the twelve Judges. After fifteen months' confinement, he sent his wife to one of the Judges, to know if a determination of his cause was near. The Judge answered, "If Mr. Gibson is in so great a hurry to know this, you may acquaint him that his cause has been, after mature consideration, finally determined, and he will not find it altogether satisfactory." His wife went back, without loss of time, and acquainted him with the information; yet he still was inattentive and careless. However, the ensuing sessions he was summoned to the bar, there to plead to his sentence, in presence of four Judges; and permission was granted to him to make his defence. It was a matter of astonishment to hear his arguments; and the many disputable points of law referred to from various books and Acts of Parliament. I believe it was the universal opinion of the assembly that he would be immediately cleared, as none of the Judges were able to confute him. At length, Judge Perrot rose from his seat, and, addressing Mr. Gibson, told him, that his crime had been well considered by the twelve Judges, and that they unanimously considered him guilty; adding, "My brethren here maintain the same opinion." Mr. Gibson, on hearing this, turned as pale as death, and was scarcely able to stand. He was then committed to his cell, and closely confined. Here I may venture to observe, his attention to my exhortations was serious and constant, although he was almost incessantly busied with other gentlemen, who attended him in his cell, drawing up some writing or other to those whom he or they thought most expedient, in order to obtain a respite or pardon from His Majesty. When the report came down that he was included in the death-warrant, he was alarmed, and began to be in earnest, inquiring of me what he must do to be saved. I applied those passages of Scripture at first which were the most awakening to his conscience. When I perceived his soul was in extreme anguish, then I pointed him to the Lamb of God, who is ever waiting to be gracious to every returning prodigal; I also applied those healing portions of God's word which seemed most conducive to his present and eternal happiness. The awful day came whereon he was appointed to die; nor did I perceive any token of a change in his soul. On going to the place of execution, his mind was greatly agitated; eternity appeared awful beyond conception; yet no one could be more diligent in making serious inquiries of what might be most beneficial to his immortal spirit. When we arrived at the fatal spot, he turned to me, being greatly terrified, and said, "O, Mr. Told, I beseech you give me all the assistance you possibly can!" which God enabled me to do, and in consequence, he appeared to be much more composed and resigned to his fate. I hope our Lord and Saviour was propitious to his never-dying soul. I endeavoured to be equally serviceable to all the rest, who were apparently in a better state to leave this world than Mr. Gibson.

I shall now speak of a few of the cutters among the

weavers: three of them I shall mention in particular, viz., Doyle, Valine, and Messman. The night Messman was brought to Newgate in order to be fettered, he discovered me at some distance; and approaching me, he said, "Mr. Told, I know you very well;" and added, crying, "I am afraid I shall suffer;" he therefore hoped I would attend him both before and after his trial, and give him all the instruction I was capable of. I accordingly imparted to him such pieces of instruction as he seemed to stand in most need of; and although he was a man of undaunted spirit, handsome, and of a tolerable good understanding, yet he was soon brought into subjection to the Father of spirits; and every visit I afterwards paid him he gave fresh evidence of deeper conviction of sin, a clearer knowledge of himself, his deep fall from God and his lost state. His conversion was very singular, being quickly changed from darkness to light and from the power of sin and Satan unto God; which was evidently perceived by all around him. Before I conclude with Mr. Messman, and his calm and peaceable exit, I judge it no wise improper, but rather necessary to render an exact account of Doyle and Valine, who were executed on Bethnal-green, by the decree of Government, and in the shrievalty of Alderman Townsend and Sawbridge.

I have but two remarks to make concerning them, nor can I represent any thing considerable respecting their attention to the things of eternity. It is true, a few favourable circumstances appeared in their behaviour; and, at Mr. Doyle's request, I wrote two or three petitions to His Majesty, and twice obtained a respite; but afterwards an order arrived to send them away for execution. Here I endeavoured to persuade Mrs. Doyle to carry another petition; but she replied with a ridiculous unconcern, "There is no occasion for it; I am very clear he will not die." By what I gathered after this, the woman's meaning was, he would assuredly be rescued by the weavers upon their arrival at Bethnal-green; and, without doubt, these were the secret intentions of the riotous mob, as was soon realized by a watch-word, which on a sudden spread all over the Green. Stones then began to fly from every quarter. Now, as I was with the officiating Ordinary in a coach, a messenger was despatched from the Sheriff, giving my companions in the coach to understand that no time for prayers would be allowed them, neither would there be any occasion for either of us; that as soon as the gibbet, which was in the cart with them, was come to the place appointed, they were to be launched off immediately. Mr. Valine, greatly terrified, begged heartily that one prayer might be offered up to God for them; but that not being granted, they were turned off in the utmost hurry and confusion.

Mr. Messman, and other of the cutters, were shortly after executed at Tyburn; but Messman, apprehensive that the weavers intended to rescue him, and he being very happy in his soul, addressed himself, when in the cart, to the spectators; saying, with a loud voice, "Good people, I humbly entreat you to keep as much silence as possible. We wish to go to our everlasting homes in peace and quietness; being happy enough to leave this world, without the least desire of living any longer in it." Nor did we endure any tumult any part of the way, or at the place of execution. Their behaviour was truly serious: from which I have much reason to believe that they are at rest from sin and sorrow, and are become partakers of everlasting glory.

I shall next give a brief account of Mr. Bolland, a Sheriff's officer, who had frequently attended the malefactors at Tyburn. He was condemned for forging an endorsement on the back of a promissory note. His character was also in many other instances sadly stained; so that the consideration of the latter, added to the former offence, together with an observation made by one of the Judges, on the frequency thereof in the mercantile world, proved the transaction too weighty to keep him upon sufficient grounds for self-vindication; otherwise, I have been informed, the mere forgery itself would not have been heavy enough to bring him, by impartial justice, to so awful a situation.

When Bolland first found that his life was closely pursued, he immediately refunded the money; yet the prosecutors would by no means deliver up the note. He informed me that his prosecutors then exacted of him a second payment of the money; and, finding his life still in danger, he paid that also, upon their giving him an indemnification under their hands, obliging themselves to cancel the indorsement; and as he was persuaded they would act upon principles of honour, he therefore paid no further attention to their proceedings; however, they refused at last to efface the indorsement.

His trial came on, and he was cast, and then committed to his cell, where he lay a long time, but gave very little attention to his soul's eternal welfare. His poor wife took every opportunity to make all the interest she possibly could. When the death-warrant came down, and Mr. Bolland was included therein, he was so engaged in writing petitions, &c., that he neither could nor would set apart a few moments for prayer and self-examination; which gave me great uneasiness. I frequently told him how dangerous his state was, while so anxious about his temporal concerns, when his soul was entirely neglected. He made many promises, but performed very few of them. A day or two previous to his execution, his wife waited on their Majesties at the play-house, where she gave a petition into each of their hands. His Majesty, in consequence of the petition, sent for the Recorder, and told him he had a great inclination to spare Bolland's life. The Recorder replied to His Majesty, that if he spared his life, whose character was truly infamous and baneful, he would spare as great a villain as any in the nation. It must be observed, I speak this only from the information received.

On the morning of the execution I went early to the cell, and laboured very much with Mr. Bolland, who betrayed a violent agitation of mind. When we had entered the chapel he discovered the most serious attention, and was well pleased to hear instruction.

As he had very little knowledge of the way to eternal life, so he was the more intent upon, and earnest in searching after, those passages of Scripture which might furnish him with any hopes of being saved. The Ordinary, myself, and other spiritual friends, used our utmost endeavours to assist him in the road to eternal life. When he was in the cart, going to the place of execution, he scarcely ceased a single minute in asking me what he must do to be saved; and at the crisis of his dissolution, he repeated the same. I can only leave him to a merciful Redeemer, hoping he is safely lodged in the arms of His love.

The next of whom I would speak was a young gentleman, Mr. Slocomb, who was executed for defrauding his father of three hundred pounds in the stock of the South Sea House: much of the gentleman and scholar were evident in the behaviour of this youth. Upon his father's coming up to London to receive his interest money, he was informed that his son brought his draft for three hundred pounds, which money he received, and the sum was debited to his father's account. Mr. Slocomb, senior, declared he never gave his son any such draft, and therefore insisted upon the receipt of his whole interest. The gentleman at the office acquainted his father, that if he would not abide the loss, they must be under the necessity of apprehending his son, who would most assuredly suffer death. The father would by no means suffer the loss; accordingly the youth was apprehended. He was afterwards condemned, and received sentence of death. The lump of adamant (his father) then retired to the country, nor would he after that see or hear from his son; neither did he once write to him, or give him any kind of advice, or remit him any relief, notwithstanding he lay a long time under sentence, before he was ordered for execution. There was something remarkably amiable in his conduct; an entire resignation to the will of God, which kept down every murmuring thought, and entirely prevented his making any complaint against the severity of his father.

His behaviour during his confinement also was admirable, being filled with perfect seriousness and devotion, as he never neglected to attend on the means of grace at every opportunity. Mr. Powell, a young gentleman who was sentenced at the same time for forgery, became a companion of Mr. Slocomb's; they constantly conversed together about the awful things of eternity, and were both truly instructive to other malefactors. They were both much lamented by all who knew them, even the most distant of their acquaintance. As their whole demeanour was grounded on the basis of godliness, they in the awful hour mutually exhibited so excellent a measure of that happy spirit, that I am firmly persuaded those who closely examined their conduct when on the brink of eternity, could entertain no doubt of their eternal acceptance with God.

The next account I shall give, is that of Mary Piner, who was sentenced to death for setting fire to her master's house. At the same time three or four men were cast for death, with whom Mary showed herself very wanton; but they appeared to be on their important guard every moment of their confinement, behaving with much penitence and contrition of spirit; therefore the enemy of their souls could not inject the fatal poison into the minds of those, by the means of Mary's ungovernable folly. I strove to make this young woman the greatest and first object of my visit, but experienced various repulses from her. I was grieved to behold her heedless conduct, especially as the death-warrant had just arrived, wherein she was included. Therefore, I took her aside, and said to her, "Mary, how is it that you, above all the other malefactors, are so regardless about your precious and immortal soul? Do not you well know that God's all-seeing eye penetrates your every action? Are you not afraid of going to hell, seeing you are in a short time to appear before the great Jehovah, against whom you have sinned with a high hand? Are you determined to destroy your own soul? Are you in love with eternal perdition and God's wrath, that you so madly pursue it? Do you long to be involved in the bottom-less pit, and the lake that burns with fire and brimstone, which will never be quenched? O! remember, if you die in your present condition, you will die eternally under the wrath of an offended Saviour; and all these miseries will be your portion for ever!" She paid particular attention to what I said; and replied, "Mr. Told, I have had some knowledge of you, having many times heard you preach at West-street chapel." At this I was astonished, and asked her why she had been guilty of so heinous a crime as setting fire to her master's house, and afterwards robbing him of his property. She answered, the devil was too powerful for her in the temptation. I now perceived a change in her countenance; nor did I afterwards hear one unbecoming expression, or observe an indiscreet action in her, to her last moments.

The night prior to her execution, I importunately be-sought her to spend every moment in wrestling mightily with God for pardon through His dearly beloved Son. To which she answered, "God being my helper, I am determined not to close my eyes in sleep the whole night." Similar advice I gave to all the rest of the malefactors, one of whom espoused the like resolution. I then desired the inner keepers to lock them all up in one cell, that they might pour out their joint supplications to the awful and tremendous Judge of the quick and dead, in whose presence they must all unavoidably appear in a few fleeting moments. This was readily granted; so they accordingly devoted that night to an inexpressible advantage, by praying, singing hymns, and rejoicing, the Lord God Himself being evidently in the midst of them. When I returned to them the next morning, after having received this soul-reviving information, I begged the keepers to unlock the cells, and lead them down into the press-yard. The first that came out was Mary Piner. I was struck with delight when I beheld the happy change in her countenance.

As she came out of the cell, she appeared to be filled with the peace and love of God, and, clapping her hands together, she gave a triumphant shout, with these words, "This night God, for Christ's sake, has forgiven me all my sins; I know that I have passed from death unto life, and I shall shortly be with my Redeemer in glory." When the service and sacrament were concluded, they all came down from the chapel, and were ordered into the press-yard room, where I continued praying for, and exhorting them all, nearly the space of forty minutes, when directions were given to bring them out, and place them in two carts. Mary Piner, accompanied by two other malefactors and myself, went in the first cart, while we went on our passage to the place of execution, I frequently exhorted them to keep the eye of their mind steadfastly looking up to Jesus, using many repetitions of some passages of Scripture, which I considered best adapted to their awful situation. Here I am strongly persuaded my labour was not in vain. She continued in this happy state, singing, praising, and giving glory to God without intermission, till she arrived at the gallows. She then accosted one of her fellow-sufferers, who cried, vehemently, in great anguish of soul, "Lord Jesus, forgive me my sins! God be merciful to me a sinner;" and said, "Do you believe that Jesus Christ died for you?" He replied, "Truly I do." "Then," said she, "there is no room to doubt of your salvation." This produced a revival of his spirit, which continued till his last breath.

When the cart was put under the gallows, she turned round to an innumerable assembly of people, saying, "Good people, I doubt not but many of you are greatly affected at beholding so young a creature as I brought to this shameful end; but, O, I am happy; having full assurance that I shall live with Him who died for me, and there commence an everlasting banquet of happiness at His right hand in the region of bliss." She then began to strengthen her fellow-sufferers, beseeching them not to doubt of the readiness of God to save them. And I hope they all received that salvation which was purchased by the blood of the everlasting covenant.

I shall now give a plain account of Mrs. Brownrigg, in order to furnish my readers with a view of her disquietude and shocking situation during her imprisonment; the Right Honourable the Lord Mayor having been pleased to favour me with an order to Mr. Akerman (the keeper of Newgate) for granting me permission to attend her while confined therein, for the cruel and wilful murder of her apprentice girl, Mary Clifford, September 4th, 1767.

I went to her accordingly, on the evening subsequent to the above direction, and was conducted to the room where Mrs. Brownrigg was sitting on her bedside, accompanied by a poor woman. I addressed her in the most awful manner I was capable of; telling her that I came in the name of the Lord Jesus Christ; and if she would accept of my services, I should consider it my duty to speak my mind as closely as possible, as I had heard very dreadful accounts of her conduct. She replied, "Mr. Told, I am very glad to see you; and shall not esteem you my friend if you do not deal with plainness towards me, and speak as closely as you can." Happy was I to hear her speak thus, and said to her, "Mrs. Brownrigg, you are in an awful situation before man, but more especially before the Almighty God; your most secret sins are within His immediate view, so that you can hide nothing from His all-seeing eye. Your character also, in the eye of the world, is rendered loathsome and horrible, as you are charged with crimes of the deepest dye, many of which I can hardly credit. However, matters appear too evident with regard to the fact of which you are accused." I likewise told her, "I very much feared she had but little mercy upon her late fellow-creatures; that she had cruelly used the deceased repeatedly, and for some length of time." Her answer was, "I acknowledge this accusation, so far as to have given the girl repeated corrections, but no further; my intentions being directly opposite to any kind of violence." I then observed to her, that I did not believe she was stimulated by so fierce a spirit of anger as to be driven to the immediate perpetration of murder; but I added also, "What were your ideas of the dreadful consequences which must issue from such shocking acts of cruelty, too shocking to nature?" She replied, "Sir, if I had any consideration of the danger, I could not have done the deed; the devil reigned with a fatal mastery over me." I then told her, the word of God expressly declares, "Whoso sheddeth man's blood, by man shall his blood be shed;" therefore I had no doubt but that her life would go for the life of the poor child. She replied, "I have no doubt of it neither." Here I began to be more pointed, and said to her, "If you are thus conscious of your guilt, there is no time to lose: immediately then lay your dreadful case before God, under a deep sense of the sin you have committed, and not for that only, but for all and every of your actual sins, from the earliest period of your life to the present moment, or you can have no just hopes of mercy at the hand of God, through the merits of a crucified Redeemer; as we are confidently assured He came into the world to save us *from* our sins, not *in* them:" therefore I continued to insist upon it, unless she humbled herself under the mighty hand of God by a heartfelt repentance, and an open acknowledgment of those flagrant crimes she had been guilty of, no favour could be afforded to her unhappy soul by the hand of God in the day of judgment, nor would she consequently have peace of mind while on earth. "This," said Mrs. Brownrigg, "I firmly believe." I then further added, "That I did not come to extort any confession from her, and begged she would confess nothing to me; but I observed to her, "You will, in a few days, be brought upon your trial, when you will not only be in the presence of the Judge and jury, but also in the more immediate presence of the all-seeing God; and witnesses will be called for to give evidence against you; then more especially will it be the time when it behoves you to speak the truth; and I charge you, therefore, at the peril of your soul, not to advance anything against the dictates of your own conscience in covering your crimes, the guilt of which you know before God you are not exempt from; but I pray you adhere firmly to the truth, should death be the consequence." She replied, "I intend it." I again advised her to reject, as much as possible, the suggestions of the enemy in covering her crimes, but be frankly ingenuous in the acknowledgment thereof before proper Magistrates. I then closed my first visit with prayer, after having given her, agreeable to her solicitations, all the spiritual assistance within the limits of my capacity. When finished, I parted with her; and the next day (being Sunday) I visited her again about twelve o'clock, asking her how she found herself, as I perceived her spirits to be greatly depressed. She replied, "Mr. Told, since you were with me yesterday, I have deeply weighed your kind instructions, which has occasioned great uneasiness and distress in my mind; and notwithstanding I was somewhat easy and composed at certain periods before, I am, alas! quite otherwise now; for I am horribly afraid. My grievous sins have been set in array before me; and I am dreadfully intimidated and fearful, lest God should never show me His mercy." I told her I was happier with this report, and much more satisfied with her present state, than at my former visit, as her conscience was now convinced of her crime. I applied many threatening as well as healing passages of Scripture to her conscience; which she very willingly, and with much thankfulness, received. I concluded this visit also with prayer, and then parted.

Upon my third visit (which was on Monday) I found her in a very bad and dangerous spirit. Here I exerted myself in order to settle her mind, and strengthen her confidence in God; but, to my disappointment, I observed that the enemy had so buffeted her soul, that she strongly endeavoured to conceal her guilt, telling me, with bitterness of spirit, she never intended murder; and that she was assured the rigid, partial jury, who sat upon the body of the deceased, would, through their envenomed prejudice, treat her with a degree of rigour and severity much heavier than her deserts. This she spoke with much warmth.

I then told her this perverseness of spirit would prove exceedingly hurtful to her precious, never-dying soul, and that it betrayed in her an absolute blindness and hardness of heart; so that no signs of repentance appeared, or the least concern for such repeated acts of violence. I likewise gave her to understand, that I considered it a grand point of my duty to defend the characters of those gentlemen who were on the coroner's inquest; adding, "Can you, Mrs. Brownrigg, entertain a thought that those gentlemen, who are under an oath, and in no wise interested in giving false evidence against you, would endeavour to take away your life, without substantial reasons and good grounds in their evidence?" I insisted upon her laying aside all such vain pretences, which were artifices of the devil to destroy her soul; telling her withal, if she would stand open to conviction, and behave in her short moments as became one who was thus confined to a few hours only, for the working out her salvation with fear and trembling, God would show her favour at the last; and the blood of Jesus Christ, which speaketh better things than the blood of Abel, would wash away the stain of that blood she had so cruelly shed. I likewise pointed out to her the loving spirit of a dying Saviour, who, when He was expiring on the accursed tree for man's redemption, prayed with His last breath, saying, "Father, forgive them; for they know not what they do." His prayer was heard and answered. When Peter was preaching to a great number of them, they were cut to the heart, and cried out in an agony of spirit, "Men and brethren, what must we do to be saved?" Peter answered them, "Repent, every one of you, and be baptized in the Name of the Lord Jesus, for the remission of your sins, and you shall receive the gift of the Holy Ghost; for the promise is unto you and to your children, and to those that are afar off, even to as many as the Lord our God shall call; therefore," I observed, "if the mercy of God extended itself to the very murderers of His only begotten Son, no doubt but it will reach your poor guilty conscience also. If you, like them, are pricked to the heart, and cry earnestly to God for mercy, through the Son of His love, you likewise shall obtain the remission of your sins, and your name shall be written in the Lamb's book of life. Then you shall sing the new song to God and the Lamb, who hath redeemed us with His blood, and saves the vilest and chief of sinners." These with many similar exhortations having been given her, she began to be more composed, never after attempting to justify herself, or even to extenuate her guilt. I concluded this visit with prayer also, and had not an opportunity of seeing her again, until the day prior to that appointed for her to die.

On the 13th of September, being the Lord's day, I came to Newgate about twelve o'clock, and met her as she was coming down stairs from the chapel. The keepers informed me of the strict orders they had received to lock her up immediately in her cell, and desired me to take notice of her behaviour. Mrs. Brownrigg then went into her cell, and I followed her, and, at her request, the turnkey and woman who attended her were both dismissed. The cell doors were then locked and bolted upon us, when she began to express the extreme anguish of her soul, saying, "Mr. Told, God for ever bless you; sit down by me." When we were seated, she began to wring her hands in vehement agitation of spirit, praying most earnestly that God, for Christ's sake, would have mercy upon her poor guilty soul; expressing herself, with floods of tears, to this effect: "O Lord Jesus, wash away the guilt of the blood which I have shed in Thy most precious blood! O Lord, I am the vilest and chief of sinners: be gracious, be merciful to me, O heavenly Jesus! for no such a sinner as myself ever existed. O save, save and deliver from eternal burnings, my poor, guilty, wretched, and hell-deserving soul! O Lord, what must I do to be saved? Gracious God, what must I do? Now, heavenly Jesus, cleanse Thou my stains, or I am undone for ever!" Thus she continued for some minutes, and then turned to me, and said, "Mr. Told, what must I do? My soul is in bitterness and heavy distress." She added also, "I wrestled all last night with God in prayer, except the space of an hour, during which I soundly slept, and had many very comfortable visits from the Lord. During my interval of sleep I dreamed a dream, in which I beheld a man coming towards me, with a glass of wine in his hand, who bade me drink it. I took particular notice of the wine that it was red; so that when I awoke I was much refreshed; and all my comforts are gone again: therefore I am now more distressed than ever."

I replied, "Mrs. Brownrigg, I am afraid you do not sufficiently permit the Spirit of God to convince you of the enormity of the crime for which you are condemned. Are you condemned in your own conscience? Do you judge yourself, that you may not be judged of God? Condemn yourself, that you may not be condemned in the day of judgment, when the secrets of all hearts will be open to God, angels and men. Do you call to remembrance the sins of your whole life? And are you fully convinced that you deserve to be punished eternally for your impiety and transgression?" She replied, "I do." "Then," said I, "if it be so, you are not far from the kingdom of God." Wringing her hands in an agony of spirit, she said, "O that I may know this! O that I may be assured of this!" She continued to use several repetitions thereof. I then asked her whether she was never tempted to destroy herself. She answered, "Mr. Told, I am glad you have asked me this question, and I will answer it without reserve. When," said she, "I was first taken to Wandsworth, the constable compelled my landlady to search my pockets, to know whether I had a knife, or any other instrument, whereby I might have committed the shocking act of suicide. I was searched accordingly; and although I had a knife secreted, yet it was not found. This threw me into a violent temptation, and I cut a small hole, the bigness of a silver groat, in the peak of these my stays. Herein," continued she, "I put the knife; it being a clasped one, I conveyed it round my hip, through the covering of my stays." After that she added, "Now as I have advanced thus far, I should be to blame were I to conceal the rest; therefore I shall acknowledge to you, Mr. Told, that many times I used to consider in what part of my body it would be most expedient to stab myself, that by so doing I might effect the business at once; yet the Lord in His infinite mercy led me safe through this temptation."

I then asked her if she had ever seriously considered the consequence of so rash an attempt, and what would have become of her soul if she had died in the act of self-murder, as it would be utterly impossible for her to be saved, not having time for repentance. She answered, "I never was inclined to think on anything of that nature; for the consideration of the shame and ignominy that are always consequent on Tyburn executions suppressed every other serious and calm reflection." I told her I had a few questions more to ask her, and begged she would return me the plain, simple truth, so that her veracity might be unsullied and spotless. She replied, "Mr. Told, I can open my heart to you, like as to myself: ask what you judge proper, and I will, by openness and simplicity, endeavour to afford you satisfaction." I then informed her, it was currently reported, and well nigh in every one's mouth, that in the course of her practice in mid-wifery she had been guilty of destroying several children in the birth, and feeding her swine with them. I added, "Is this true or not?" She replied. "I was asked the same question some time ago by an eminent Physician; but truly, Mr. Told, I never had any misfortune during the time of my practice, except with three; and I now desire you to take down, in writing, the names of those three gentlewomen I then laid, and they will give you a satisfactory account; namely, whether the fault lay at my door or not, as they were all three brought into the world putrefied. I have had," said she, "as good success in general as most women in my calling, and was equally esteemed by my employers; neither were they ever so wonderfully astonished as at the time this unfortunate affair came to light." The names of the three gentlewomen who had the dead children, were Mrs. Gore, at Camberwell; Mrs. Plude, at the workhouse in Grub-street; and Mrs. ———, at the Bell Inn, Holborn.

The second question I asked her arose from an information I had received touching her secret transactions with seventeen apprentice girls, whom she had, at several times, acquired from various parishes in and about London; as it was said, that when she was requested to give an account of them, she could produce but three. I demanded, "Is this true or not?" To which she answered, "I never in my life had more than three apprentices, viz., the deceased, the evidence, and one that is gone back to the Foundling Hospital."

I then asked her, if she could say, in the presence of Almighty God, that she never practised any of those cruelties before. Her answer was, "I never did." I asked her what could induce her to commit so dreadful an act of barbarity? She replied, "About ten years ago, when I had six small children about me, I walked closely in the ways of God, rising at five in the morning, and going to six o'clock prayers: then, Mr. Told, I was very happy in my God, who manifested Himself to me, so that I walked stedfastly in the light of His blessed countenance for a considerable time: but O! unhappily for me, I grew slack in my duty, forsook my God, and He forsook me; so that I fell into the spirit of pride and anger, and then into the crime for which I am to die. I can give you, Mr. Told, no other reason; but I beg you will help my poor distressed soul all that you can." I replied, "I humbly hope God will be your helper, protector, and defender." As I still hoped she had not committed the unpardonable sin against the Holy Ghost, I trusted there was yet room for mercy; therefore I pressed upon her to understand, that Christ Himself declared that every other sin, of what nature or kind soever, shall be forgiven unto men upon true repentance and deep humiliation, under a deep sense of guilt before God. Here I exhorted her to come to the throne of grace, and trust in the blood of the everlasting covenant; and said that God, for Christ's sake, would in no wise reject or cast out those who came to Him through the Son of His love; but would blot out all their iniquities as a cloud, and their transgressions as a thick cloud; and that God was in Christ, reconciling the world unto Himself. I also told her, that the Lord Jesus, even while He hung upon the accursed tree, bore all our sins on His own body, saying, "It is finished;" having made a full, sufficient sacrifice, oblation, and satisfaction for the sins of the whole world, for hers and mine in particular: that we were not damned so much for certain crimes committed, as for not believing in the great truths of the Gospel; which tells us, "God sent His Son into the world not to condemn the world, but that the world through Him might be saved."

Again I informed her that when the Lord Jesus sent His twelve disciples, He gave them this command, "Go ye into all the world, and preach the Gospel to every creature." "By the Gospel you are to understand," said I, "the glad tidings of salvation, through a crucified Redeemer: whosoever therefore believes, and is baptized, shall be saved; but he that believeth not shall be damned." "My dear woman," added I, "venture your all in time and eternity on this great Saviour of the world; and then, though your sins be as scarlet, God will make them white as snow; and although they be as crimson, they shall be as wool. You see, then, that God's thoughts towards us are not as our thoughts towards Him and one another. See then that you lay fast hold on this hope of eternal life set before you: and though you will assuredly to-morrow, before this time, pay the debt of your natural life for the life you have destroyed; yet be of good comfort, the Son of God hath given body for body, and soul for soul, that we may be made partakers of eternal life, and be for ever where the wicked cease from troubling, and the weary spirits are at rest."

Thus I continued to press the doctrine of salvation by faith with weight upon her conscience; and found my labour was not in vain. She began to be much comforted before we parted, and found she could now trust body and soul in the hand of her dear Saviour.

Her countenance was much altered; and that languid gloom which rested upon her at our first entrance into the cell, I easily perceived to terminate in pleasant serenity. Composure of mind, and resignation of spirit, were expressed strongly in all her looks. I then went to prayer, and parted with her for this time, commending her into the hands of a merciful Redeemer.

Monday, the 14th instant, being the day of her execution, I went to Newgate about a quarter past six o'clock in the morning, and found her with the Rev. Mr. Moor, the Ordinary, in the press-yard room. We went immediately up to chapel, endeavouring to comfort her in the best manner we could; and found her spirit fully prepared to receive instruction, her mind greatly composed, and her heart filled with prayer.

When we came to the chapel, we tarried some time before the prayers began, in the course of which interim the turnkey had introduced Mr. Brownrigg and their son. They addressed each other in a very striking manner; then the Ordinary prayed extempore with them, after which we sang a hymn; he then exhorted and prayed again. When he had done, he desired me to pray. I did so; and we sang another hymn, very applicable to the dying malefactor's case. Now when we were ready to communicate, the others were admitted up to the chapel, among whom were three Clergymen, who joined us in the sacred supper of our Lord; (and truly a blessed time it was, especially with the malefactor, her husband, and son;) at the close of which solemnity it was considered prudent to dismiss every person from the chapel, in order to give them the fairer opportunity of taking their last farewell of one another. So we all retired accordingly; but I had not reached the bottom of the steps before the keeper beckoned to me, saying, Mrs. Brownrigg desired to speak a few words with me. I speedily returned to her; upon which she said, "Mr. Told, we want you to employ a little more of your time with us; pray give my husband and son a word of advice." I did so, agreeable to her desires, and imparted, I may venture to say, no small share of instruction; for which they returned me many thanks. I then addressed myself to Mrs. Brownrigg, as she was in the spirit of prayer. While I was speaking to her the son fell down on both his knees, and bursting into a flood of tears, with his head against his mother's side, said, "I beseech you, my dear mother, lay both your hands upon my head, and bless me!" She replied, "I hope God will bless my dear son." Almost frantic, he added, "My dear mother, put both your hands upon my head, and bless me yourself." His mother then put both her hands upon his head, saying, "My blessing be upon thee, my dear child." The husband then fell down on both his knees on the other side, saying, "The Lord bless you! God be with you, my dear wife!" being scarce able to speak for weeping. He assured her that all the care that was possible should be taken of her offspring, that they might be trained up to serve God. They then parted, when the keeper and myself led her down stairs (as she was, through extreme debility, unable to walk alone,) and carried her into the press-yard room.

The Sheriff not having arrived, we caught another opportunity of being useful to her, applying our short time to the most advantage. A Clergyman belonging to St. Paul's was likewise of excellent service, in giving her good and wholesome advice.

The time came when Mrs. Brownrigg was ordered into the cart, when the Rev. Mr. James and myself stationed ourselves by each side of her, Mr. James on the right hand, and myself on the left. When we had fixed ourselves, I perceived the whole powers of darkness ready to give her a reception. Beckoning to the multitude, I desired them to pray for her;

at which they were rather silent, until the cart began to move. Then they triumphed over her with three huzzas, which was followed by a combination of curses.

When we had passed through the gate, carts were placed on each side of the street, filled principally with women. Here I may say, with the greatest truth, nothing could have equalled them, but the spirits let loose from the infernal pit; and, to be brief, this was the spirit of the wicked multitude all the way to the place of execution.

Notwithstanding her crime was horrible, yet God, in His infinite mercy, supported her mind: seeing her time was short, she did not make one complaint against such treatment; neither did she drop a murmuring expression from her lips in any part of her passage. I repeatedly asked her, if the dreadful tumult did not draw the attention of her mind from off the Lord Jesus. She replied, "Not in the least; I bless God." Then some of the common cries from the thoughtless concourse, accompanied with dreadful imprecations, were, "Pull off her hat, that we may see the b——'s face." However, I withstood this cutting clamour all the way, till we came to the place of execution, and that for two reasons; first, I was conscious it would too much expose her to the censure of the inexorable mob, and, which was abundantly worse, it would discompose her mind, and hinder her meditating on God; the second consideration was, that, as the incensed mob thought it was not enough to rejoice over her by common rage and defamatory abuse, but were so cruel as to cast stones, dirt, &c., therefore, if I through endeavouring to pacify them by a friendly address, should, on the contrary, excite their madness and exasperation, they would not only disturb her mind, but endanger her life before the law had executed its office. I must observe here, I never in the course of my life, beheld so much the absolute necessity which all the Ministers of the Gospel, of every denomination, lay under, in plucking those brands from eternal death and destruction.

When we arrived at the place of execution, the outcries of

the mob were not so violent; yet, when she was tied up, to the fatal tree, and exposed to God, angels, and men, (an awful spectacle,) little or no compassion was shown by the populace.

After the executioner had tied her up, I discovered a horrible dread in her countenance, and begged to know the cause. She said, "I have many times passed by this place, and always when near it a dreadful horror seized me, for fear that one day I should be hanged; and this enters my mind afresh, and greatly terrifies me!" I said, "Your mind all the way was very composed, and you told me you could put your full trust and confidence in your Redeemer; and that you had no doubt but that you should be happy with Him: don't you find it so still?" She replied, "I still retain my confidence; but what I frequently imagined, whenever I passed this piece of ground, now occurs, and therefore I am exceedingly terrified." I then told her it was not her duty to pay any attention to that; and encouraged her to look steadfastly to the Lord Jesus, and that would be sufficient to subdue every other opposition, and enable her to resign her spirit into the hands of Almighty God.

Some time before she was turned off, the Ordinary came into the cart, spake to her, and prayed with her. We sang two hymns, and continued to exhort her for three quarters of an hour. She was very devout, crying vehemently for mercy.

Just as the cart was ready to draw off, I turned to her, and advised her, in her last moment, to keep her mind steadfastly fixed upon Christ. She said, "I hope I shall." The cart then drew off, and I humbly trust God received her departed spirit.

* * *

Thus concludes the narrative of the life of Mr. Silas Told, written by himself, some time before his departure from this vale of tears, after having passed through a troublesome and laborious life with great fortitude and patience; being continually anxious for the good of his fellow-creatures, particularly the condemned malefactors in the several prisons in and about the metropolis; striving ardently, by all the means in his power, to promote their everlasting welfare; submitting meekly, for Christ's sake, to the ill treatment which he too often experienced, not only from prisoners and keepers, but to reproach from those who ought rather to have encouraged and applauded him. After having done all the good in his power, he cheerfully resigned his soul into the hands of his heavenly Father, in December, 1779, in the sixty-eight year of his age, and hath, no doubt, received this blessed welcome, "Well done, good and faithful servant, enter thou into the joy of thy Lord."